To Bob Wallace and Valentino Balboni, who always knew what a Lamborghini ought to be. —SC

In memory of my father, David Mann, who gave me my love of cars. —JM

Brimming with creative inspiration, how-to projects, and useful information to enrich your everyday life, Quarto.com is a favorite destination for those pursuing their interests and passions.

© 2022 Quarto Publishing Group USA Inc.
Text © 2015, 2022 Stuart Codling
Photography © 2015, 2022 James Mann except where noted

Second edition published in 2022
First Published in 2015 by Motorbooks, an imprint of The Quarto Group,
100 Cummings Center, Suite 265-D, Beverly, MA 01915, USA.
T (978) 282-9590 F (978) 283-2742 Quarto.com

All rights reserved. No part of this book may be reproduced in any form without written permission of the copyright owners. All images in this book have been reproduced with the knowledge and prior consent of the artists concerned, and no responsibility is accepted by producer, publisher, or printer for any infringement of copyright or otherwise, arising from the contents of this publication. Every effort has been made to ensure that credits accurately comply with information supplied. We apologize for any inaccuracies that may have occurred and will resolve inaccurate or missing information in a subsequent reprinting of the book.

Motorbooks titles are also available at discount for retail, wholesale, promotional, and bulk purchase. For details, contact the Special Sales Manager by email at specialsales@quarto.com or by mail at The Quarto Group, Attn: Special Sales Manager, 100 Cummings Center, Suite 265-D, Beverly, MA 01915, USA.

26 25 24 23 22   1 2 3 4 5

ISBN: 978-0-7603-7659-1

Digital edition published in 2022
eISBN: 978-0-7603-7660-7

Formerly found under the following Library of Congress Cataloging-in-Publication Data
Codling, Stuart, 1972-
Lamborghini supercars fifty years : from the groundbreaking Miura to today's hypercars / Stuart Codling ; photography by James Mann.
pages cm
ISBN 978-0-7603-4795-9 (hc)
1. Lamborghini automobile--History. I. Title.
TL215.L33C63 2015
629.222--dc23
        2015004630

Cover Design: Cindy Samargia Laun
Front Cover Image: James Mann; Frontis: Lamborghini
Page Design: Karl Laun
Photography: All images courtesy Automobili Lamborghini S.p.A. and James Mann unless otherwise indicated.

Printed in China

LAMBORGHINI 60 YEARS

STUART CODLING | PHOTOGRAPHY BY JAMES MANN | FOREWORD BY VALENTINO BALBONI

CONTENTS

ACKNOWLEDGMENTS 6

FOREWORD *by* Valentino Balboni 7

INTRODUCTION Birth of the Bull 8

CHAPTER 1 **MIURA:** The World's First Mid-Engine Supercar 20

CHAPTER 2 **GOING MAINSTREAM:** Supercar Performance for the Family 42

CHAPTER 3 **COUNTACH:** Supercar Poster Boy 56

CHAPTER 4 **RAISING THE ROOF:** Coming to America 80

CHAPTER 5 **DIABLO:** The Supercar Refined 90

CHAPTER 6 **MURCIÉLAGO:** Audi Flexes Its Muscle 112

CHAPTER **7**	**GALLARDO:**	
	The Driver's Supercar *130*	
CHAPTER **8**	**REVENTÓN:**	
	Exclusive Performance *148*	
CHAPTER **9**	**AVENTADOR:**	
	Recalibrating the Supercar Formula *158*	
CHAPTER **10**	**SESTO ELEMENTO:**	
	All the Power, None of the Weight *178*	
CHAPTER **11**	**HURACÁN:**	
	The Future Is Now *194*	
CHAPTER **12**	**THE LEVIATHANS:**	
	Introducing the "Rambo Lambo" *214*	
CHAPTER **13**	**TO THE FUTURE PAST:**	
	Remake, Re-imagine, Reboot *224*	
INDEX	*238*	

ACKNOWLEDGMENTS

AUTHOR'S ACKNOWLEDGMENTS

Thanks to James Mann, for tirelessly chasing down some of the rarest Lamborghinis on earth; Kevin Wood, for furnishing access to the LAT Archive and reserving the Jim Clark mug; Zack Miller at Motorbooks; and to my wife, Julie, for her love and support throughout.

PHOTOGRAPHER'S ACKNOWLEDGMENTS

Thanks to car owners Geoff Armstrong, Peter Blake, John Britton, Lynne and Richard Bull, Ian Cartlidge, Jeremy Copp, John Lawler, Gareth Meatyard, Gareth Richardson, Stephen Ward, and Tommy Wareham at Supervettura; Fazel Adabi, Kevin Fisher, Maria-Cristina Guizzardi, Juliet Jarvis, and Martina Tacchella at Lamborghini; Fabio Lamborghini, Tonino Lamborghini, and Francesca Poggioli at Museo Lamborghini; Valentino Balboni, Martin Buckley, Giles Chapman, and Ian Dawson for extra archive images; and Marc Bogard, Simon Hutson-Flynn, Kevin Lees, Dougal Macdonald, and Jane Weitzmann at JHW Classics.

FOREWORD
BY VALENTINO BALBONI
LAMBORGHINI CHIEF TEST DRIVER

I started working at Automobili Lamborghini on April 21, 1968, after completing a mechanic's school.

I began as a mechanic's apprentice, helping senior mechanics and learning from them how to repair and take care of the cars.

My time with Automobili Lamborghini became a perfect, instinctive mix of passion and work which lasted my entire career—it was a respectful devotion.

I was lucky to be there at the right time. The company was growing day by day. Founder Ferruccio Lamborghini was with us often, and one of his great skills was knowing how to motivate and encourage everyone around him to feel like an important part of the company's life.

Ferruccio hired young engineers recently graduated from university because he knew that they were excited to show up and develop something outstanding, which wasn't otherwise available at that time in the high-performance sports car world. He was right!

He always wanted to offer better performing cars than his competitors. With the success of the first production models, he created a new vision of how an exclusive sports car should be, embodying at the same time his own character and temperament.

I always had due respect and appreciation for our historical competitors and neighbours, but Automobili Lamborghini wanted to break the common rules and move forward in outrageous new directions, creating an image and exclusivity which always distinguished the founder and Lamborghini owners.

The Miura definitely started a new era in our world and forged a new path, making Automobili Lamborghini well-recognized and appreciated worldwide.

The aggressive and intimidating design of the Countach is still unique and even in modern times represents Lamborghini's open-mindedness while still challenging the concept of smoothness and comfort for a modern sports car. These are just two of many models that define Lamborghini's history.

Lamborghini's heritage and passion are still present in the works of art currently rolling out of the Sant'Agata Bolognese facilities. I am sure the roots are deep enough to guarantee long life and joy to Lamborghini enthusiasts and owners. The distinction that is Lamborghini will be always there.

Enjoy *Lamborghini 60 Years*.

Valentino Balboni

INTRODUCTION
BIRTH OF THE BULL

Ferruccio Lamborghini built his fortune and reputation on manufacturing tractors in the aftermath of World War II. He also turned healthy profits by making pneumatic valves and air-conditioning units.

The exact wording of the ill-tempered exchange between Enzo Ferrari and Ferruccio Lamborghini that prompted Lamborghini to become an automobile manufacturer in his own right—if, indeed, the conversation happened at all—is steeped in myth. And yet it is so delightfully plausible that it has remained central to Automobili Lamborghini's origin story for more than 50 years and five changes of ownership after the fact—or unfact, if you're determined to remain cynical.

Ferruccio Lamborghini came from humble stock, but he was already a successful entrepreneur, with a diverse portfolio of businesses that included a tractor manufacturer, an air-conditioning supplier, and a pneumatic valve fabricator, when he decided to join the automobile industry in the early 1960s. This was a boom period for prestige, high-performance carmakers, and it would have been perfectly natural for Ferruccio to launch his own brand even if he had not become disenchanted with Ferrari's approach to aftercare.

But myth is a vital element of brand mystique. It's what has persuaded many different people, over the course of the past 50 years, to buy and cherish wildly impractical and often temperamental beasts bearing the logo of the bull. So let us allow Ferruccio to tell his own story in his own words, as related in a 1991 interview in *Thoroughbred & Classic Cars* magazine:

> After I got my first Ferrari, my other six cars—Alfa Romeo, Lancia, Mercedes, Maserati, Jaguar were always left in the garage. In 1958 I went to Maranello for the first time to buy a 250GT coupe, the two-seater by Pininfarina. After that I had one, maybe two, 250GT Berlinettas, the short-wheelbase car from Scaglietti. I did like that one very much. It was ahead of its time, had a perfect balance and a strong engine. Finally I bought a 250GT 2+2, which was a four-seater by Pininfarina. That engine was very strong too and it went very well.
>
> All my Ferraris had clutch problems. When you drove normally, everything was fine. But when you were going hard, the clutch would slip under acceleration; it just wasn't up to the job. I went to Maranello regularly to have a clutch rebuilt or renewed, and every time, the car was taken away for several hours and I was not allowed to watch them repairing it. The problem with the clutch was never cured, so I decided to talk to Enzo Ferrari. I had to wait for him a very long time. "Ferrari, your cars are rubbish!" I complained. Il Commendatore was furious. "Lamborghini, you may be able to drive a tractor but you will never be able to handle a Ferrari properly." This was the point when I finally decided to make a perfect car.

Ferruccio Lamborghini was the youngest of five children, born in the farming town of Renazza di Cento on April 28, 1916. Astrologically inclined readers will recognize that date as falling under the sign of Taurus, the bull, believed to confer characteristics of strength and determination. As a teenager he grew more interested in the mechanics of the machines that worked the land than in the process of working the land, and it is said, though not recorded, that he enrolled in a technical college (most likely Bologna's Fratelli Taddia) to study engineering.

In 1940, at age 24, he was called up by the Italian Air Force and served as ground crew on the Aegean island of Rhodes, helping to maintain the fleet stationed there. With three military airfields and a strategic location, Rhodes was both an important base and a major target, especially as Italy drifted toward surrender following the downfall of Benito Mussolini in July 1943. Rhodes came under attack by both Allied and German forces during the Dodecanese campaign of September 1943, falling initially to Germany and then occupied by Britain after Germany surrendered in 1945. Lamborghini spent several months as a prisoner of His Majesty's Government.

Owners have come and gone, but Lamborghinis continue to be built on the same site in Sant'Agata Bolognese. Ferruccio chose it because it offered plenty of room for expansion—and he got favorable breaks from the local government.

Ferruccio returned home to a smashed economy. Automotive plants and other engineering concerns had been given over to munitions manufacture, machinery had been cannibalized or melted down to make war machines, and there was widespread hunger and stagnation. But there were also opportunities, with many of those great machines of war now unused and ripe for repurposing, and worn-out agricultural machinery needing to be repaired or replaced. Ferruccio established a tidy little business maintaining clapped-out farm vehicles and snapping up army surplus to remake into new ones; and, as the supply of ex-military machines naturally began to dry out, he formed Lamborghini Tractori SpA to build new vehicles from the ground up, including their engines.

In tandem with this, Ferruccio enjoyed tinkering with road cars and modified several 569-cc Fiat Topolinos for himself and other customers. With one, bored and stroked to 750cc, he entered the 1948 Mille Miglia road race, but didn't complete the course. "I finished my Mille Miglia in an *osteria* [pub]," he said, "which I entered by driving through the wall."

Through the 1950s Lamborghini became one of Italy's largest tractor manufacturers, and it made Ferruccio a wealthy man. But he wasn't done. In 1960 he established another business, Lamborghini Bruciatori SpA, building air-conditioning systems for industrial and domestic use, and later in the decade, after the founding of Automobili Ferruccio Lamborghini SpA, he would open another lucrative sideline: Lamborghini Oleodynamica SpA, a manufacturer of pneumatic valves.

In Lamborghini's own origin story, after the possibly apocryphal exchange with Enzo Ferrari, Ferruccio attended to his car's unsatisfactory clutch himself, as he related in the *Thoroughbred & Classic Cars* interview:

> To start with, I bought a bigger clutch from Borg & Beck and had it fitted in the tractor factory workshop. Then we discarded Ferrari's

cylinder heads, which were rather simple affairs with just a single overhead camshaft and 12 rockers. I had them replaced by heads of our own design with twin cam shafts. We then put the engine back in the 250GT and fitted six horizontally mounted carburetors, just like on the 350GT two years later. It was already quite a good car.

Several times I used to wait for test drivers from Maranello, with Prova MO plates on their cars, at the entrance to the motorway near Modena. After some time we would be doing 230, 240kmh [145–150mph] and then I would start to pull away from them—my Ferrari was at least 25kmh faster than theirs thanks to our four-cam conversion. "Hey, Lamborghini, what have you done to your car?" they would ask me later. "Oh, I don't know," I used to answer with a grin!

As a businessman and successful entrepreneur, Ferruccio would not have entered a high-stakes game such as prestige automobile manufacture only to avenge a snub. The truth was that there was money to be made if you got it right. As he himself alluded to in a 1964 interview with *Sporting Motorist* magazine, there was a gap in the market for this: "In the past I have bought some of the most expensive gran turismo cars and in each of these magnificent cars I have found some faults. Too hot. Or uncomfortable. Or not sufficiently fast. Or not perfectly finished. Now I want to make a GT car without faults. Not a technical bomb. Very normal. But a perfect car."

That was the aim as he filed the paperwork to found the car company in 1962 and entered negotiations with various financial institutions and local authorities to build a new factory. While these deals were being done, he gathered a useful cluster of young and talented engineers to head up development of the prototype car in the tractor factory: Paolo Stanzani, Giotto Bizzarrini, and Gian Paolo Dallara.

Building the new factory in Sant'Agata Bolognese, near Ferruccio's other businesses, made sense from an oversight point of view, and since the area was impoverished he had no difficulties securing permission from the Communist-controlled local authorities to build on a Greenfield site. Likewise, labor costs would be cheap, though a shortage of the necessary skills would force him to outsource some work. He was also able to offset his own personal financial exposure by obtaining a long-term, interest-free loan from the local government, on condition that the factory was staffed by members of the sheet-metal workers' union. This latter deal would come back to bite him several years down the line.

Lamborghini commissioned Franco Scaglione to style the prototype's body, which would be built in Turin by Sargiotto (Carrozzeria Touring took over for what would become the production 350GT). According to Bizzarrini's account, he showed Ferruccio drawings of a 1.5-liter quad-cam V-12 Formula 1 engine he had designed and received a commission to build a larger version that would be more powerful than its Ferrari equivalent. It has subsequently been written that Bizzarrini went off-piste and delivered a full-on racing engine, which led to Bizzarrini's split with Lamborghini, but others—including Dallara—have said that Ferruccio had not yet decided whether he wanted a fast-road engine or one more competition oriented.

It has also been claimed, by no less an authority than the learned L. J. K. Setright, that Bizzarrini's engine never made it to production and that the resulting V-12 was actually designed in secret by Honda. He adumbrated this theory in a 1986 article in *Supercar Classics* magazine.

> The accepted legend is that the original engine was designed for Lamborghini by Bizzarrini, based on a design study of his for a 1.5-liter Grand Prix engine which (properly, from what I remember of it) came to nothing, and that this was subsequently modified or mollified by Dallara. Now I will admit to a good deal of respect for the work of young Dallara, but honestly I cannot see anything in the work of either of these engineers, either before or since, of comparable quality. I am therefore all the more inclined to believe what I was privately told quite authoritatively in 1975—that the design was secretly commissioned by Lamborghini from Honda. . . . There was no other engine, and especially no other V12, of equal merit created in the decade before the debut of the first Lamborghini, nor any superior in the years immediately following other than by Honda. What more appropriate than that one of the world's best engines should be designed by the world's best engine maker?

It is true that Honda entered Formula 1 with an intricate 1.5-liter V-12 engine in 1965, and that there are some common features—particularly the siting of the inlet tracts between the camshafts rather than inside the *V*—which are unusual. But the story seems far-fetched and predicated on anonymous sources and wishful thinking—which, for a confirmed Honda lover such as Setright, was not in short supply. More prosaically Bob Wallace, Lamborghini's longtime test driver, dismissed the notion as "crap."

The 3.5-liter all-aluminum V-12 was advanced for its time, featuring double overhead cams (though a multi-valve head would not grace it until the 1980s) for each cylinder bank, driven by a duplex roller chain and actuating inverted bucket-type cams. The wet-lined block had a classic 60-degree *V* angle, with a seven-bearing crankshaft and hemispherical combustion chambers. The piston crowns featured a pronounced dome, although extant engineering drawings show that flat-headed pistons were also considered. Bizzarrini specified a dry sump and six Weber downdraft carburetors and claimed a power output of around 360 brake horsepower, and the engine would be displayed in this form at the Turin motor show in late 1963. By then Bizzarrini had departed the project and Dallara was reworking the V-12 with a wet sump and horizontal carburetors, while detuning it for a more relaxed power delivery, in line with the prototype 350GT's character.

The 350GTV prototype also appeared at the '63 Turin show, but not with the engine inside it. Long, lithe, and elegantly simple of line, the car came together too late to

Franco Scaglione's first sketch of what would become the 350GT was wildly dramatic, and even the toned-down prototype was deemed not practical enough by Ferruccio Lamborghini.

install a drivetrain or anything but a rudimentary suspension arrangement, and the engine would not fit under the low hood. Thus, Lamborghini exhibited the V-12 separately and the prototype's hood stayed closed, concealing a payload of ceramic tiles that had been installed in the engine bay to make the front end sit at the right attitude. If any prospective customer wanted to look inside the cabin or under the hood, Ferruccio would gesticulate at a nearby employee and say, "See that idiot? He's lost the keys." Some writers have erroneously attributed these events to the first public showing of the Miura.

Ferruccio was not quite convinced by the car, and in any case Sargiotto did not have the facilities to attempt serial production, so he engaged Carrozzeria Touring to restyle it and build the bodies for the production 350GT. Touring came with impeccable credentials, having patented the Superleggera method of construction in the 1930s, but was in the process of falling on hard times after expanding to build Rootes Group-based cars, which sold poorly. The company went into receivership just as the 350GT went on sale after a successful launch at the 1964 Geneva show.

The 350GT did without the pop-up headlights of the prototype, and the build quality of the steel space frame chassis and aluminum body panels was much improved. Only 13 were made in 1964, though, so Ferruccio canned plans to introduce a smaller-engined model, and instead asked Dallara to increase the swept volume of the V-12 to four liters. He hired Bob Wallace to work on the underdeveloped and underwhelming dynamics of the cars and pushed on; the company was selling the 350GT at a loss, and Ferruccio needed to offer something bigger and more powerful to compete with the likes of the Ferrari 275.

From 1965, the 350GT was offered with a larger 3,929cc engine and sold as the 400GT. But with coachbuilder Carrozzeria Touring in financial trouble, only 23 were built.

350GT

Chassis	Steel tube frame
Suspension	Independent double wishbones front/rear, coil springs, telescopic shock absorbers, anti-roll bars
Brakes	Unventilated Girling discs
Wheelbase	2550 mm
Front/rear track	1380 mm/1380 mm
Wheels/Tires	15 in × 6.5 in, Pirelli Cinturato 205/15
Engine	Front longitudinally mounted 60-degree V-12
Bore/Stroke	77 mm/62 mm
Cubic capacity	3464 cc
Compression ratio	9.5:1
Maximum power	275 bhp at 6500 rpm
Valve gear	Dual overhead camshafts, chain drive, 2 valves per cylinder
Fuel/ignition system	6 Weber carburetors, Bendix pump, 2 coils and distributors
Lubrication	Wet sump
Gearbox	ZF 5-speed
Transmission	Rear-wheel drive
Clutch	Dry single-plate, hydraulically assisted
Dry weight	1297 kg
Top speed	155 mph

400GT

Chassis	Steel tube frame
Suspension	Independent double wishbones front/rear, coil springs, telescopic shock absorbers, anti-roll bars
Brakes	Unventilated Girling discs
Wheelbase	2550 mm
Front/rear track	1380 mm/1380 mm
Wheels/Tires	15 in × 6.5 in, Pirelli Cinturato 205/15
Engine	Front longitudinally mounted 60-degree V-12
Bore/Stroke	82 mm/62 mm
Cubic capacity	3939 cc
Compression ratio	10.2:1
Maximum power	320 bhp at 6500 rpm
Valve gear	Dual overhead camshafts, chain drive, 2 valves per cylinder
Fuel/ignition system	6 Weber carburetors, Bendix pump, 2 coils and distributors
Lubrication	Wet sump
Gearbox	ZF 5-speed
Transmission	Rear-wheel drive
Clutch	Dry single-plate, hydraulically assisted
Dry weight	1380 kg
Top speed	155 mph

Touring, though running in administration, took on the build of the four-liter 400GT, which had a longer chassis and steel body panels, and the company also made two drophead examples of the 350GT. Zagato presented a pair of cars based on 400GT running gear in 1965, but Ferruccio, though he was reportedly pleased by their appearance, elected to focus on the 400GT as Lamborghini's mainstream model. In 1966 the definitive 400GT arrived, with a resculpted floorpan to allow a pair of small rear seats, and Lamborghini's own gearbox and differential in place of the original ZF running gear.

By then, though, Lamborghini's attention was turning to something a little more special. In all, 120 350GTs would be made, as well as 23 400GTs and 224 400GT 2+2s, but while these solidly engineered grand tourers found fans, they were not nearly as exciting as the car Lamborghini was about to unleash: the Miura.

Giotto Bizzarrini (left, with Ferruccio Lamborghini and Gian Paolo Dallara) designed the prototype V12 engine but Dallara was responsible for making it roadworthy.

OPPOSITE: Ferruccio Lamborghini may have sold the company in the early 1970s, but he remains a crucial element of the Automobili Lamborghini story and takes pride of place in the museum.

GIOTTO BIZZARRINI

Legendary engineer Giotto Bizzarrini enjoys a reputation as founder of one of the great lost marques in the pantheon of Italian exotica. Born in 1926 and a graduate in mechanical engineering from the University of Pisa, he would have somewhat complicated and tempestuous relationships with some of his employers. However, he played a key role in the genesis of many much-loved racing machines, as well as building a limited number of cars under his own name.

Bizzarrini's iconoclastic nature meant he never lingered over one project for too long. After a short stint at Alfa Romeo in the mid-'50s, he joined Ferrari in 1957 as a test driver and engineer, taking a hand in engine research as well as chassis development. Maranello cars bearing his stamp include the legendary short-wheelbase 250GT as well as the 250GTO.

In 1961 Bizzarrini was among the number of Ferrari staff who left to found the ATS racing marque bankrolled by Count Volpi di Misurata. Alas, ATS proved short-lived, largely because Volpi lost interest when its projects failed to deliver decent results.

The offer from Lamborghini therefore came at the right time and was one of Bizzarrini's first freelance projects after he set up on his own Società Autostar. Accounts differ, but Bizzarrini himself has claimed that he showed Ferruccio designs for a 1.5-liter four-cam V-12 Formula 1 engine he had designed and was instructed to "make it as big as Ferrari's three-liter." He has also claimed that an agreed bonus if he exceeded horsepower targets went unpaid until he pursued Lamborghini through the courts.

Bizzarrini's involvement with Lamborghini was brief—he said he took the engine from sketch to prototype in four months—and he moved on to work with Iso on the Rivolta and Grifo models. Following a disagreement with Piero Rivolta in 1966, and further court proceedings, Bizzarrini secured the rights to build a development of the Grifo under his own name. These Bizzarrini 5300 Stradas are now exceedingly rare—only 110 were built—and coveted.

The company went bankrupt, but Bizzarrini continued to freelance and work in academia, while also building a handful of concept cars under his own name.

PAOLO STANZANI

Paolo Stanzani had a hand in developing the Miura and, after taking over as technical director from Gian Paolo Dallara, led the engineering of the Countach.

The 400GT 2+2 was a likeable grand tourer but was outshone by Lamborghini's more exciting models.

Born in Bologna in 1938, Stanzani joined Lamborghini not long after his contemporary, Gian Paolo Dallara. Stanzani came from resolutely working-class stock—his father was a truck driver—and this would inform his practical and financially prudent engineering outlook throughout his career. Having studied engineering at Bologna University, Stanzani gained an introduction to Ferruccio Lamborghini and was taken on as Dallara's assistant in 1963.

Five years later he succeeded Dallara as chief engineer, developing the Urraco and supervising the improvement of the Miura into its final SV form. He would also play a pivotal role in the creation of the Countach, including the innovative reversed configuration of the engine and gearbox, before leaving in 1975. Later in life he would become the chief engineer at the reborn Bugatti and oversee the Gandini-designed EB110 supercar.

Stanzani's role in keeping the company afloat during the turbulence of the early 1970s should not be underestimated, though it is difficult to corroborate some of the claims—not least by Stanzani himself—that Ferruccio stepped back from day-to-day management of Automobili Lamborghini as early as 1967, placing full responsibility in Stanzani's hands.

The 350GT prototype excited interest at the 1963 Turin Show, but Lamborghini was not convinced by the styling. *Martin Buckley*

MARCELLO GANDINI

Though a quarter century has elapsed since the last launch of a Gandini-styled Lamborghini, the Piedmontese master craftsman will forever be associated with the raging bull thanks to his role in the creation of the Miura, Countach, Diablo, and many prototypes, as well as less extreme Lamborghinis such as the Urraco and Espada. The son of an orchestra conductor, Marcello Gandini was born in 1938—the same year as the man he would ultimately replace at Nuccio Bertone's studios, Giorgetto Giugiaro.

It was at Bertone that he made his name, sculpting the adventurous and dramatic Miura for Lamborghini, then beginning a long dalliance with wedgy angularity that would give the world the Lancia Stratos, the Lamborghini Countach, and the Fiat X19. He is perhaps less well-known for his work on mainstream European cars such as the Citroen BX—arguably the last of the genuinely *outré* cars to bear the double-chevron logo—the first-generation BMW 5-Series, and the Renault Supercinq.

Though Gandini remained in Bertone's employ for 14 years, he felt undervalued, and during interviews he has alluded to some rancor in their relationship. As a freelance designer, Gandini was considered one of the preeminent aesthetes of the 1980s, as his Countach design refused to date. Today he still works from a drawing board rather than a CAD terminal and remains busy, though happy to remain out of the public eye.

Marcello Gandini. *Ian Dawson*

MIURA

THE WORLD'S FIRST

IN 1965 LAMBORGHINI WAS A COMPANY IN FAST-FORWARD MODE. Perhaps too fast. Production was barely getting going for the 350GT, a car that, as Gian Paolo Dallara noted, had been rushed into manufacture without adequate testing and still had many faults to iron out. But Lamborghini's young and ambitious engineering team pressed on. In November 1965 they would unveil a car at the Turin show that would stop everyone in their tracks—even though it didn't have a bodyshell yet, or a name.

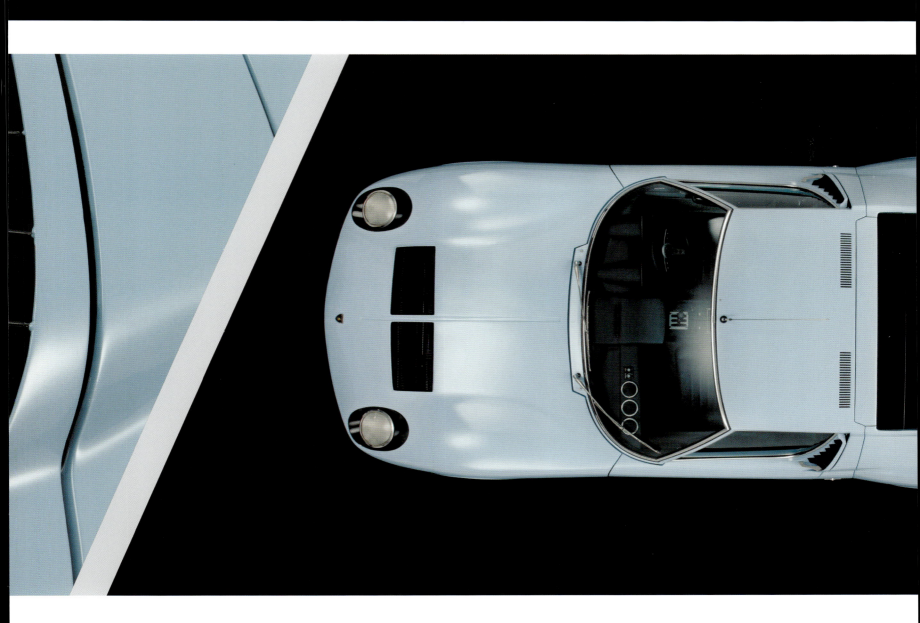

MID-ENGINE SUPERCAR

Myth has it that the Miura was developed behind Ferruccio Lamborghini's back and presented to him as a *fait accompli*, but many of the project's principals have denied this.

The rolling chassis unveiled at Turin and badged P400 was every bit as alluring as the body that would ultimately clothe it, and clearly derived from race car thinking: a steel central monocoque "tub" with three longitudinal box-section members, drilled for lightness and joined together by the floor and bulkheads at each end; similar box-sections extended front and rear to cradle the engine and provide suspension mounting points. The Bizzarrini V-12 engine was mounted transversely behind the driver and slightly ahead of the rear wheels, with the transmission and differential sharing an intricate one-piece casting—and the engine oil. Ferruccio, it's said, proudly exhibited the rolling chassis to showcase Lamborghini's engineering prowess. It did the job. In 1965, with the exception of the low-volume De Tomaso Vallelunga, the ATS 2500GT and René Bonnet Djet, the only high-performance cars with mid-mounted engines were the participants in Enzo Ferrari's ongoing battle on-track with Henry Ford II.

Accounts differ as to the manifesto of Lamborghini's senior engineers—Dallara, Bob Wallace, and Paolo Stanzani. Were they, as has been claimed, trying to cajole Ferruccio into dropping his longstanding objection to building an outright performance car instead of elegant grand tourers? Was this rolling chassis intended to be the thin end of the proverbial wedge?

The three men had worked on the initial chassis designs outside of office hours. It was when Dallara approached Ferruccio with the proposal, in order to secure a development budget, that he was directed to turn it into a mid-engined road car. The rapturous response to the rolling chassis at Turin sealed the deal. Lamborghini had orders in the book, and a procession of coachbuilders beating a path to his stand wanting the honor of creating the bodyshell. With the company's preferred coachbuilder, Carrozzeria Touring, already insolvent and operating in administration, Ferruccio farmed out the styling of the new car to Bertone of Turin with a view to showing a complete car at Geneva the following March; a nervous Nuccio Bertone had waited until the final day of the show before approaching with his pitch. Dallara was instructed to collaborate closely with Bertone's new designer, Marcello Gandini.

While Gandini is now credited with the design of the car, there are nuances to the story. He joined Bertone in November 1965 to replace Giorgetto Giugiaro, who had left to join Ghia; and in a 1996 interview in the authoritative *Classic & Sports Car* magazine, Giugiaro claimed, "Gandini took my sketches and finished the car—70 per cent of the design is mine." He produced a number of design studies dated October to November 1964 that featured some common elements with the final Miura, as evidence of his assertion.

This story has bobbed into view many times since then, with Giugiaro proving a not entirely reliable witness, and a more recent investigation by *Classic & Sports Car* revealed further nuances that bear retelling. Giugiaro went on record in *Automotive News Europe* in 2008 to say, "Gandini designed the Miura and I have never said anything different to this simple statement, so I have nothing to deny." This backtracking was possibly a result of a legal threat to the magazine after an earlier article on the Miura's genesis in which it published one of the controversial drawings. Then in 2012 the British magazine *Car* published an article in which Giugiaro produced the sketches once again and told the author, "Since I left some drawings there, maybe he saw them—I don't know."

The Miura's compact steel monocoque "tub" was advanced compared with Lamborghini's competitors—Ferrari included—and featured strategically located holes to lighten the structure.

Giugiaro has said that the sketches were for a project for Bizzarrini, but there is no record of this having actually been commissioned, and his own assistant at Bertone, Piero Stroppa, cannot recall seeing them at the time. Accounts vary as to when Giugiaro actually left, but Stroppa has confirmed that the tenures of Giugiaro and Gandini did not overlap and that Stroppa had the studio to himself for some time before Gandini started on November 1.

Bertone did the deal with Lamborghini at the Turin show, and Stanzani recalls, "In the first meeting, Dallara and I expressed to Marcello Gandini our points of view on how our new car should be and in particular what we had in mind for the body: a race car for the road! We mentioned the Ford GT40 because that was the *non plus ultra* at that time. A few days later, Gandini presented some sketches and renderings of his styling proposal. Ferruccio and all of us were enthusiastic and did not want any changes."

Dallara concurs that when they were shown Gandini's proposal, on Christmas Eve 1965, "the drawing was approved immediately" and the only changes made subsequently were details. Legend has it that Ferruccio's response was simply, "Make it."

Classic & Sports Car's investigation concluded by inviting a clutch of well-respected stylists to compare Giugiaro's sketches with the finished car, most of them sharing the view that there were few really significant features or proportions in common. One, preferring not to be named, said: "The designer of the century cannot come to terms with the fact that the design of the century isn't his work. Without doubt the Miura is the work of Marcello Gandini and Giugiaro had nothing to do with it."

Regardless of parentage, the bodyshell that was uncovered at Geneva in March 1966, bearing the Miura badge for the first time—named after Eduardo Miura, whose fighting bulls had inspired Lamborghini's logo—caused a stampede. Painted a dazzling (and soon to become iconic) orange, the beautifully balanced coupe styling was complemented by strikingly unusual features, such as the pop-up headlights with their black "eyelashes." On the prototype these rose with the headlights; wisely, Lamborghini dropped this from the production model.

Here was a car—an outrageously low car at that, just 43 inches high—that looked like nothing else on the road. One-piece nose and tail panels showcased the best in Italian craftsmanship as well as—in theory—offering excellent access to the engine bay, luggage compartment, spare wheel, and fuel tank. In practice, hefting these substantial pieces of metal aloft was a challenging task that required much practice, finesse, and some strength.

Quite apart from its shape, the color and detailing of the Miura would have a profound effect on the automotive world, as L. J. K. Setright noted in his book *Drive On! A Social History of the Motor Car*:

> What made the Miura look even more striking was its color, one that had surely never been seen on a car before, even at a motor show: tantalisingly poised somewhere between yellow and orange, it became

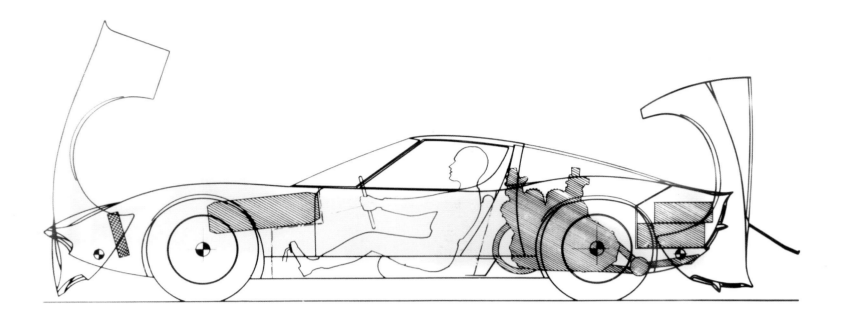

This side elevation reveals just how close the driver's head is to one cylinder bank of the transversely mounted engine.

in the next few years the most compellingly fashionable color—first for sporting cars, eventually for everything—ever to take over the motoring scene, in varying interpretations from Positano Yellow to that sunburnt orange which distinguishes western Texas.

The Miura had a further and more lasting influence on fashion. Cleverly offsetting that extraordinarily positive color was the ultimate in negativity, matt black: it was applied to everything—window surrounds and wiper arms, mirrors and grilles, louvers and lamp-rims—that might conventionally be polished or plated. Again the industry at large was keen to copy: it took time to find black coatings that would stay matt and not chip or flake off, but in the end it was a useful production economy. The public was not at all indignant about the cheapening of their cars, where once there had been costly chromium or stainless steel, because the public had been told that non-reflective black was safer in that it did not cause dazzle.

For such a radical car to progress from rolling chassis to stage unveiling within four months was remarkable, so it's no surprise that myths have grown up around it. A frequently recounted story has it that the Miura on the stand at Geneva had a shaming secret: the engine bay was empty, save for some ballast to persuade the rear of the car to sit at the correct height. Supposedly, in the rush to complete the prototype, somehow nobody had thought to check that the engine would fit in its allocated space until it was too late; therefore, the engine bay remained locked throughout the show, though Lamborghini's sales chief, Ubaldo Sgarzi, secured enough deposits for the Miura and the 400GT for production to go ahead.

Scoop photographs taken by Peter Coltrin after the prototype had been shipped from Bertone's workshops to Sant'Agata, and which were featured on the cover of

Bertone's unique Miura Roadster made its first appearance at the Brussels auto show in 1968. Some Miura owners have been tempted to convert their own cars to achieve a similar appearance over the years, perhaps inadvisably.

Road & Track magazine, do show the prototype sitting rather high at the rear. But Nuccio Bertone has subsequently gone on record to say that he drove the prototype to Geneva himself. The most likely explanation is that myth and the effect of passing time on genuine memories has led to the 350GT prototype's launch being blurred with the Miura's.

But was the wider market ready for this car? At this point nobody at Lamborghini could be sure the Miura would sell in great numbers. Before the show, Ferruccio, Dallara, Bertone, and Sgarzi had each written on a piece of paper how many they expected Lamborghini to sell in the coming year. Bertone wrote five; Dallara wrote 100; Ferruccio 20; and Sgarzi 50. Just as pressing a concern, perhaps, was how many Lamborghini could actually make.

By early 1966 the workforce at Sant'Agata had expanded to nearly 300, but serial production of the Miura did not begin until the final months of the year. There were quality hurdles to overcome, and the compressed design and development process of the car was made very obvious by the curious ergonomics of the interior, where controls looked as if they had been packed in wherever they could fit. The driver had to work two switches to activate the lights, for instance—one near the gearlever to raise them, and another in the roof panel to toggle them on and off. And provided all the driver needed to know was how fast he was going and what revs the engine was spinning to, he was adequately served by the instrument panel in front of him. Everything else was jostling for position in a central binnacle.

Bertone built and painted the bodyshells in Turin and shipped them down to the factory, where they were mated to the chassis and trimmed. The first four Miuras off the line were retained for testing and development under Bob Wallace's eye, but even then, as Dallara has said, "Our customers were the test drivers." A number of eccentricities made it through to regular production, including a tendency for the carburetors to flood, setting the whole engine bay alight. The steering was heavy and the broad, swooping nose generated chronic lift at high speeds, making the outer echelons of its performance envelope a place to be explored only by the most skilled and fearless.

"Anyone who has achieved a true 170mph in a Miura can tell you that the effect experienced is that of a jet plane on a runway (complete with imminent take-off!)," noted Joe Sackey in *The Lamborghini Miura Bible*, "and the relationship between man machine and God's green earth at that speed is a fragile one, compressed time-travel if you like, only to be undertaken by those brave souls who dare. You haven't lived until you've tried it . . . some say."

Even so, by the end of 1967 more than 100 Miuras had been delivered to customers—many of whom, it must be said, quickly had the interior re-trimmed to a higher standard. Only one other mid-engined rival—the Ford-engined De Tomaso Mangusta—had entered serial production, and it was far less extreme. Lamborghini had the market almost to itself.

At the Geneva show in '67, Lamborghini demonstrated an extraordinary four-seater, the Marzal, based on a stretched version of the Miura chassis and riding on handsome Campagnolo magnesium wheels. Designed by Gandini, the wedge-shaped Marzal featured a smoked glass roof and a pair of huge, mostly glass doors that hinged upward from the roof, while the front and rear bodywork tipped outward, like the Miura's. Its inline-six engine was, in effect, half of the Bizzarrini V-12, and mounted slightly aft of the rear axle in order to maximize cabin space. The interior was a riot of space-age shapes. Setright described it as "perhaps the most extravagant piece of virtuoso styling to have come out of Europe since the war."

Testing revealed the car's balance was fundamentally poor, largely because of the engine's position. The Marzal had one further public outing, where Prince Rainer and Princess Grace were hustled around in it for a parade lap before the Monaco Grand Prix, before it went to the museum. Gandini folded the lessons learned into the four-seater Espada that Lamborghini would show the following year. The Marzal became a footnote to history, but a valuable one: the sole example fetched 1.5 million at auction in 2011.

Lamborghini wasn't just pressing on with the development of new cars. In 1968 it offered a revised version of the Miura, the P400S, as well as unveiling a roofless variant at the Brussels motor show. In an effort to reduce the buffeting that plagues

The original and unique Bertone-built Miura Roadster had neither roof nor side windows. The chassis was strengthened to compensate for the roof's removal, the air intakes were larger, and the rear bodywork was subtly resculpted.

the occupants of drop-top cars, Gandini subtly restyled the bodyshell and only removed the top section of the roof.

Bertone, though, required a minimum of 50 orders to commit to a production run, and while the roadster attracted plenty of interest on the stand, there weren't enough signatures in the order book by close of play. Ferruccio mothballed the idea and sold the car on to the International Lead Zinc Research Organization, who stripped it and galvanized the shell for use as a promotional exhibit. This at least ensured the sole roadster built would have a long life; it passed through several owners before being restored and repainted in metallic blue in the mid-2000s, and formed the centerpiece of a Lamborghini 50th anniversary celebration at the 2013 Amelia Island Concours d'Elegance. Some owners have had their Miuras converted into roadsters along the lines of Gandini's original design, which is perhaps not the most respectful way to treat a vehicle that is a classic in its own right.

The principal engineering changes in the P400S consisted of a stiffened chassis, constant-velocity driveshafts, and revised rear suspension, while the engine was treated to revised camshaft profiles and larger intake manifolds. These brought the V-12's claimed output to 370 brake horsepower, although there is some debate as to the veracity of the quoted figures. Still, a P400S subjected to a contemporary performance test by the British-based *Autocar* magazine yielded a top speed of 172 miles per hour and clocked 0–60 in 6.7 seconds; this at a time when the best-selling car in the UK was the Austin 1100 (maximum speed 87 miles per hour, 0–60 in 17.3 seconds).

Dallara left to join De Tomaso in 1968, and Ferruccio appointed Paolo Stanzani as technical director in his stead. Stanzani has since claimed in an interview (with

Evo magazine) that Dallara's nose had been put out of joint because Ferruccio had wanted to step back from the day-to-day operation of the company and hand control to Stanzani, Dallara's junior. Whatever the truth of this claim, trouble was brewing elsewhere in Sant'Agata.

As part of the deal to obtain tax breaks from the Communist-controlled local government when he opened the factory, Ferruccio had undertaken to allow his workforce to be fully unionized. In 1969 industrial unrest swept across Italy and, not for the last time, production at the Lamborghini factory came to a halt with a series of lightning strikes as employees walked out at their union's behest. Though Ferruccio saw it coming—he was known for mingling on the factory floor rather than residing in his office—he was powerless to stop it.

In spite of the disruption, development work continued on new models, including the Jarama and the Urraco through to 1970, when Lamborghini's engineers began to hatch plans for the Miura's replacement—but not before making the ultimate Miura, the 400SV. Launched at the 1971 Geneva show, the 400SV was a proper step forward in engineering and performance.

The Lamborghini V-12's air inlet ports are between the camshafts rather than inside or outside the V.

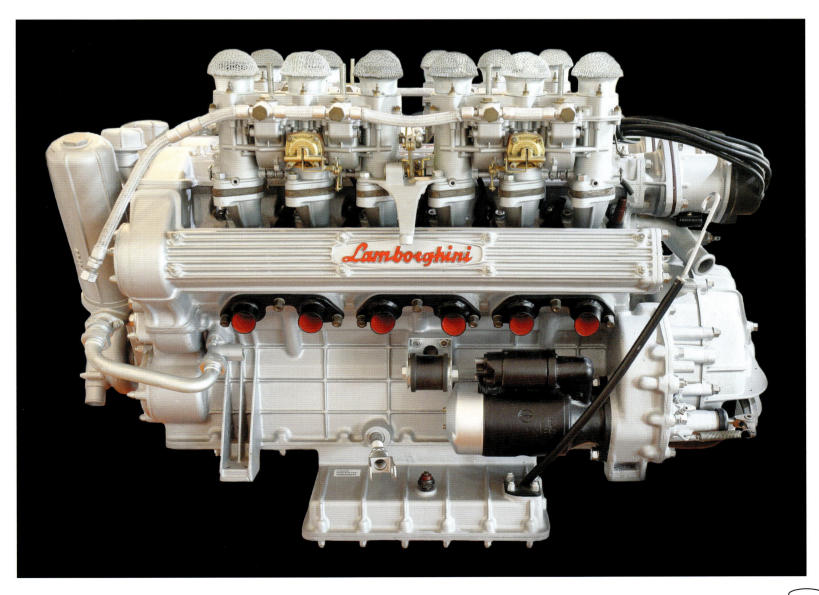

The Miura production line ran at a sedate pace; just 764 examples of this landmark supercar were built from 1966 to 1972.

While the headline power rose to a claimed 385 brake horsepower thanks to new carburetor arrangements and different cam timing, the most significant engine change came a short way into the production run with a welcome move to separate lubrication for the engine and gearbox. The transmission gained a limited-slip differential and the suspension was revised front and rear, with a five-inch wider rear track. Outwardly you could tell the 400SV apart from its predecessors by the lack of "eyelashes" around the headlamps, as well as the more muscular rear fenders.

Mark Hughes, writing in *Classic & Sports Car*, summed up the experience of driving an SV—for the keen driver, a sort of reverential fugue state:

> How exquisite the handling is. If you were to single out one mechanical element as an example of how the Miura does things, it has to be the steering. The leather-bound rim of the three-spoke wheel is slender and invites you to hold it gently, which is the right way to hold the reins of a Miura. Light in feel, fluid in movement and uncannily communicative, the unassisted rack-and-pinion system gives millimeter-perfect control and an extraordinary sense of one-ness with the car. There's none of the self-centering of modern cars, but having to unwind lock adds to the sense of complete command.

Motoring hard, but still directing the car with fingertips and palms, you feel every subtlety of road surface, tire loading and stance. No other car gives such detailed, precisely tuned messages from the world outside. . . . For a machine of such awesome performance, the Miura's refinement is such that you can genuinely imagine living with one daily. That is if you don't mind some engine noise. When you see one cylinder bank of the V12 and a pair of gigantic Weber carburetors through the Perspex panel behind the seats, you expect that progress in a Miura won't be peaceful. It isn't.

Four triple-choke carburetors, 12 pistons, four camshafts, 24 valves and one timing chain create a gnashing frenzy inches from your ears—and that's only at tickover.

The Miura's engine and transmission were cast as one piece in aluminum, and early models had a single sump.

Miura doyenne Joe Sackey put it more pithily: "Make no mistake about it: this is not a car for the squeamish, or for whiny sissies."

Total Miura production ran to 764 cars, including rebuilds of damaged ones (musician Miles Davis famously crashed his in 1972, breaking both legs as well as his Miura). Immaculate examples now change hands for telephone-directory figures; an immaculate SV that had completed only 600 miles since a full rebuild fetched $2 million at auction in Monterey in 2014.

BOB WALLACE

Obsessed with cars as a youth, New Zealander Bob Wallace moved from his native Auckland to Italy in 1960 at age 21 to pursue a tentative job offer from Maserati. He and his friend John Ohlson (according to Wallace's own account; Gian Paolo Dallara's recollection is that he arrived with Chris Amon) had both been active on the hot rod scene and acted as jobbing mechanics for the continental racing teams who visited during the European winter. Neither of them spoke Italian. It was a difficult baptism in European working practices.

Wallace found gainful employment as a mechanic with Camoradi, a racing team founded by American entrepreneur Lloyd "Lucky" Casner. Camoradi achieved great success in the early 1960s in sports car racing with Maserati Tipo 61 "Birdcage" sports-racers, with their standard of preparation and semi-works status (Maserati was undergoing one of its periodic bankruptcies) attracting the likes of Dan Gurney, Stirling Moss, and Masten Gregory.

In 1961 Wallace worked for Scuderia Serenissima, the team founded by Count Volpi, working on all manner of machinery—from Ferrari sports cars to a Formula 1 Cooper T51 raced by Maurice Trintignant (Eoin Young, press secretary to Bruce McLaren, noted an encounter with his fellow Kiwi at the Cooper factory in his diary). Volpi's relationship with Ferrari would end when he bankrolled ATS, the company founded by disgruntled ex-Ferrari workers including Carlo Chiti and Giotto Bizzarrini.

Wallace also earned a reputation as a safe and capable test driver, which set him in good stead when he joined Lamborghini's payroll in late 1963 (by this time, Ohlson had moved to America to work for Carroll Shelby). As the likes of McLaren and Jack Brabham were proving on the Formula 1 circuit, drivers with mechanical experience were incredibly valuable, and Wallace soon found himself appointed chief test driver with a staff of four.

For the development of the 350GT, Miura and Countach owed much to Wallace's engineering rigor. But these were wild times on roads that were considerably less busy than they are now.

"All the factory drivers would clock in on the autostrada toll and get a Milan-to-Modena time," Wallace told *Road & Track* in a 1998 interview. "Everyone would try to beat the record. My fastest time was 38 or 39 minutes for the 106-mile distance, averaging well over 160mph. I'd go hunting for a [Ferrari] Daytona or a [Maserati] Ghibli with *Prova* [test] plates and we'd run each other down the road. While we never compared notes on the cars, we did become fairly good friends with the Ferrari and Maserati testers."

Heading west from Italy's motorsport valley and over the mountain range that forms Italy's "spine," Wallace and his friendly rivals also engaged in an unofficial world underground speed record, as he related in an interview with *Hemmings Sports & Exotic Car* in 2008:

I don't know whether you've been over the autostrada through the Apennine Mountains from Bologna to Florence, but there's a whole series of sweeping tunnels through the mountains, and that was it. Now, whoever set the quickest clock time, from one toll gate to the next, he had the record. Back then, they had a stamp-in, stamp-out ticket with the time on it, and so forth and so on. Oh, it was a lot of fun. You look back on it, and it was actually dangerous and stupid. But that's the way it was. Crazy, but fun. Couldn't do it today in the traffic and everything. Hopefully, the country has gotten a little saner since then.

Wallace left Lamborghini in 1975, fearing for the company's future under its new owners. He handed over test-driving duties to another former mechanic, who had joined Lamborghini as an apprentice in 1968—Valentino Balboni. Initially he returned to New Zealand with his wife, but then he moved to the USA to found an automotive restoration company.

Ill health prevented him from attending Lamborghini's 50th anniversary celebrations at the factory in May 2013, and he passed away that September.

"The news of the death of Bob Wallace hit me and all of us at Lamborghini and leaves us with a great sorrow," said President and CEO Stephan Winkelmann. "As the first test driver of the company, Wallace played a key role in the early years of Lamborghini and strongly contributed to the birth of the myth of the Bull. Automobili Lamborghini is close to his relatives and friends, and will honor his memory."

Miura P400

Chassis	Steel box-section monocoque
Suspension	Independent double wishbones front/rear, coil springs, telescopic shock absorbers, anti-roll bars
Brakes	Unventilated Girling discs
Wheelbase	2504 mm
Front/rear track	1412 mm/1412 mm
Wheels/Tires	15 in × 7 in, Pirelli Cinturato 205/15
Engine	Rear transverse-mounted 60-degree V-12
Bore/Stroke	82 mm/62 mm
Cubic capacity	3939 cc
Compression ratio	10.4:1
Maximum power	370 bhp at 7500 rpm
Valve gear	Dual overhead camshafts, chain drive, 2 valves per cylinder
Fuel/ignition system	6 Weber carburetors, Bendix pump, 2 coils and distributors
Lubrication	Wet sump
Gearbox	Lamborghini 5-speed
Transmission	Rear-wheel drive
Clutch	Dry single-plate, hydraulically assisted
Dry weight	1040 kg
Top speed	177 mph

Miura P400S

Chassis	Steel box-section monocoque
Suspension	Independent double wishbones front/rear, coil springs, telescopic shock absorbers, anti-roll bars
Brakes	Unventilated Girling discs (ventilated from second phase)
Wheelbase	2504 mm
Front/rear track	1412 mm/1412 mm
Wheels/Tires	15 in × 7 in, Pirelli Cinturato 205/15
Engine	Rear transverse-mounted 60-degree V-12
Bore/Stroke	82 mm/62 mm
Cubic capacity	3939 cc
Compression ratio	10.4:1
Maximum power	370 bhp at 7500 rpm
Valve gear	Dual overhead camshafts, chain drive, 2 valves per cylinder
Fuel/ignition system	4 triple-stroke Weber carburetors, Bendix pump, 2 coils and distributors
Lubrication	Wet sump
Gearbox	Lamborghini 5-speed
Transmission	Rear-wheel drive
Clutch	Dry single-plate, hydraulically assisted
Dry weight	1040 kg
Top speed	177 mph

GIAN PAOLO DALLARA

Born in Varano de' Melegari in 1936, Dallara studied aeronautical engineering at the Politecnico de Milano after finding his original choice of university, in Parma, too limiting. When Enzo Ferrari came shopping for graduate trainees, Dallara naturally considered this too good an offer to refuse and began working at Maranello in December 1959.

After two years of focusing on stress engineering in Carlo Chiti's design department, he left to join Maserati, but in 1963 he received a call from Giotto Bizzarrini, whom he had known at Ferrari and who had been engaged to design Lamborghini's V-12 engine. Dallara duly became chief engineer at Lamborghini after just five years in the trade.

"It surprised me then and it still does surprise me that Lamborghini should ask such a young man to be chief engineer," he said in an interview in 2004. "After all, I was under 30."

One of his first tasks was to redevelop Bizzarrini's peaky and competition-focused engine into one more suited to Ferruccio's vision, as well as specifying the chassis of what would become the 350GT. Then, in collaboration with Bob Wallace and Paolo Stanzani, came the Miura. He wrote in his autobiography, *It's A Beautiful Story*:

> I had nothing else to do on a Saturday or a Sunday anyway, and had a whole factory to play around with. Let's build a lighter car to show it could be done. Have some sort of a mobile test bed for new ideas or trying something different, that sort of thing.
>
> He [Ferruccio] told me, "You can do whatever the hell you want to do as long as it doesn't interfere with your daily job." You get up and start testing at five in the morning, and drive and play around until three in the afternoon, and then go and play around trying to build something. Well, I didn't have anything better to do, and I've always enjoyed cars and still do.
>
> But as far as any serious effort to build a race car, no, no, that's something that writers and journalists and people in the past just sort of invented.
>
> Ferruccio Lamborghini's avowed intent was to produce faster and more attractive cars than Ferrari. Initially the [Miura] bodywork was to have been produced by Touring, but they were replaced by Bertone, who was also in competition with Pininfarina and Ferrari. I remember when Nuccio Bertone arrived in the factory on Christmas Eve with the original sketch: it was an immediate success, we were really impressed. And that was how one of the greatest phenomena in Italian motoring history was born.

Dallara left Lamborghini in 1968 for De Tomaso, where he designed both the road-going Pantera and a Cosworth-engined Formula 1 car, which was run by a young Frank Williams. The tragic death of driver Piers Courage—burned when magnesium in the chassis caught fire during an accident at the 1970 Dutch Grand Prix—prompted De Tomaso to quit F1 at the end of that year, and Dallara's next move was to found his own agency.

He acted as a design consultant on the Countach, but in recent years his company Dallara Automobili has carved a niche as a race car manufacturer and composite subcontractor, building successful Formula 3 and IndyCar racers and supplying the F1 feeder series GP2 and GP3.

Gian Paolo Dallara modified the power curve of the prototype V-12 and added a wet sump; horizontal carburetors enabled it to fit beneath the 350GT's low hood.

MIURA S JOTA

Ferruccio Lamborghini may not have been familiar with the old saying that the quickest way to make a small fortune in motor racing was to start out with a large one, but he shared that outlook. Though he was adamant that his marque would not participate in motor sports, he did permit Bob Wallace to develop a prototype version of the Miura during 1970 that would be eligible for GT racing. This was a moving target, since sports car racing was easily as popular as Formula 1 at the time and just as prone to snap rule changes, as the governing body sought to limit performance gains—and manufacturers continued to dance around them. Fittingly, the name Jota derives from a kind of dance thought to originate in the Aragon region of Spain, and which shares some elements with the waltz.

Wallace stripped weight from the car, including the interior trim, added roll cages to the cabin, and made extensive detail changes to the suspension geometry. He also fitted wider rear wheels (up from seven inches to nine). The most noticeable exterior difference was at the front, where the pop-up headlights were replaced by fared-in ones, underlined by a chin spoiler added to balance out the Miura's characteristic front-end lift at speed. Many of the exterior panels were formed from lighter gauge materials, including aluminum alloy. Wallace also repositioned the fuel tanks to each side of the car to improve its balance.

In the engine bay the Miura S Jota received many of the upgrades due for the Miura in 1971, including the separation of the engine and gearbox lubrication systems. Along with a higher compression ratio, this yielded a reported 440 brake horsepower at 8,000 rpm.

Wallace submitted the car as a proposal to Ferruccio but was turned down, and the prototype came close to being scrapped before a wealthy Italian enthusiast stepped in to buy it. He did not get to enjoy the car; it left the road—reportedly with his mechanic at the wheel—and hit a bridge, then set alight. Contemporary photographs reveal the extent of the fire damage.

The original Jota was not rebuilt, but some customers requested cars built to a similar spec, and Lamborghini duly obliged. From 1971 to 1974, a number of Miura SVJs (thought to be five, but some reports put it as high as seven) left the factory. These included many of the engine, drivetrain, bodywork, and suspension modifications made to the S Jota, but with the interior left intact. At least two went to German Lamborghini dealer and racing driver Hubert Hahne; another is said to have gone to the Shah of Iran and was later bought by actor Nicolas Cage.

Other replicas also exist—modified by owners from original Miuras, to the horror of purists.

Miura P400SV

Miura P400SV

Chassis	Steel box-section monocoque
Suspension	Independent double wishbones front/rear, coil springs, telescopic shock absorbers, anti-roll bars
Brakes	Twin-servo ventilated Girling discs
Wheelbase	2504 mm
Front/rear track	1412 mm/1541 mm
Wheels/Tires	15in × 7in, Pirelli Cinturato 205/15 (front); 15 in × 9 in, Pirelli Cinturato 255/15
Engine	Rear transverse-mounted 60-degree V-12
Bore/Stroke	82 mm/62 mm
Cubic capacity	3939 cc
Compression ratio	10.7:1
Maximum power	385 bhp at 7850 rpm
Valve gear	Dual overhead camshafts, chain drive, 2 valves per cylinder
Fuel/ignition system	4 triple-stroke Weber carburetors, Bendix pump, 2 coils and distributors
Lubrication	Wet sump
Gearbox	Lamborghini 5-speed
Transmission	Rear-wheel drive
Clutch	Dry single-plate, hydraulically assisted
Dry weight	1245 kg
Top speed	186 mph

GOING MAINSTREAM

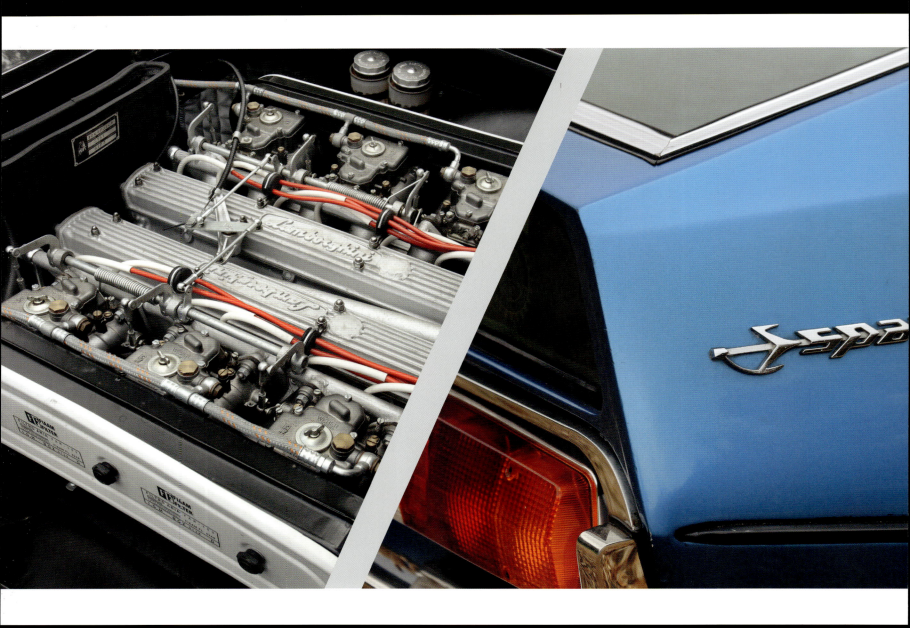

SUPERCAR PERFORMANCE

HAVING WOWED VISITORS TO THE GENEVA MOTOR SHOW, in 1966 with the Miura, and in 1967 with the futuristic Marzal concept, Ferruccio Lamborghini intended that in 1968 his company would demonstrate maturity and a more rounded model range. He had not set out to become a supercar manufacturer, and yet interest in the Miura far exceeded the public's appetite for the 350GT and 400GT, cars Ferruccio felt more in tune with his vision.

FOR THE FAMILY

MARZAL

Coming a year after the Miura's public debut at Geneva, the Marzal was no less of a showstopper but a very different kind of car, representing Ferruccio Lamborghini's ambition to create a proper long-legged grand tourer with generous accommodation for four. As such, it prefigured the Espada and Islero, albeit in a substantially more extrovert fashion. *Autosport* magazine's technical editor John Bolster described it as "incomparable" and "a supreme example of Italian art."

For Marcello Gandini, the Marzal concept represented an opportunity to properly announce his creativity to the world, given the muddied authorship of the Miura. He was unstinting in his efforts, garlanding the already outré bodyshell with huge gullwing doors, a smoked glass panoramic roof, and a futuristic interior featuring a hexagonal motif repeated elsewhere in the detailing of the bodyshell. The Marzal's prototype 2-liter inline-six engine was in effect in the rear cylinder bank of the Lamborghini V-12, and it mounted transversely just aft of the rear axle. Though the car wasn't destined for production, it featured an air-conditioning system, which would have been necessary for everyday use, given the sheer volume of glazing.

While the Marzal was based on a stretched version of the Miura's chassis, the openness of the architecture above the waistline demanded additional bracing, which made the car relatively heavy: 2,646 pounds. The trade-off to enable the smaller engine to accelerate the Marzal with sufficient verve was a low final drive ratio, which gave a top speed of 118 miles per hour, relatively modest in GT terms.

At the time, though, the Marzal's performance was somewhat less of a talking point in the press than its glazed doors; as Ferruccio himself put it, somewhat primly, "a lady's legs would be there for all to see."

Of the two new cars Lamborghini unveiled at Geneva in 1968, one would become the company's biggest-selling model over a decade in production, while the other, for all that it epitomized what Ferruccio felt a GT car should be, failed to register with its intended audience. Both are now considered Lamborghini obscurata.

The styling of the Espada—Spanish for "sword"—was again the work of Marcello Gandini, and it followed the general principle of the Marzal in that it promised to combine grand touring performance with family car accommodation and everyday practicality. It must be said the shape and detailing more closely resembled the Jaguar-based Pirana show car, also designed by Gandini (to a brief laid down by the *Daily Telegraph* newspaper) and shown at Earl's Court in 1967.

Among the challenges facing Gian Paolo Dallara was to accommodate the 4-liter V-12 in a position that would benefit the handling, since the rear-engined Marzal had proved tail-happy, and a mid-mounted location would militate against refinement and passenger space. His solution was to locate the engine up front, nearly 8 inches further forward than in the 400GT 2+2, though there the engineering comparisons between the two models ended: for the Espada, Dallara opted for a pressed-steel box chassis rather than a tube frame construction. Even so, it followed the same convoluted artisan production method in that the chassis was fabricated by Marchesi of Modena, bodied in Turin by Bertone, then returned to Emilia Romagna for finishing at Lamborghini's Sant'Agata factory. Thus, each car had completed a round trip of around 370 miles before it was showroom ready.

Though the Espada (above) bore some resemblance to the Marzal concept (opposite page), its architecture was very different, with a front-mounted engine.

At the prototype stage, the Marzal-style gullwing doors were dropped in favor of a single conventionally hinged door on each side, and a prototype German-made hydropneumatic self-levelling rear suspension system was evaluated. The rear suspension system also was ultimately discarded on account of not being refined or reliable enough, though it remained on the options list.

The opulently trimmed interior was improved during the model's life through an amendment to the chassis design, which yielded more rear headroom, and the Marzal-style hexagon-themed instrument panel was tidied up in the Series II Espada, introduced in 1970. Power steering became standard in the Series III car from 1973 onwards in response to criticism from some quarters. In all, it's believed 1,217 examples were built until production ceased in 1978, making the Espada the most prolific seller of this phase in Lamborghini's history, even if it goes largely unrecognized by the mainstream audience today.

Espada

Chassis	Steel semi-monocoque
Suspension	Independent double wishbones front/rear, coil springs, telescopic shock absorbers, anti-roll bars
Brakes	Ventilated Girling discs
Wheelbase	2650 mm
Front/rear track	1490 mm/1490 mm
Wheels/Tires	15 in × 7 in, Pirelli Cinturato 205/15
Engine	Front longitudinally mounted 60-degree V-12
Bore/Stroke	82 mm/62 mm
Cubic capacity	3929 cc
Compression ratio	9.5:1
Maximum power	325 bhp at 6500 rpm
Valve gear	Dual overhead camshafts, chain drive, 2 valves per cylinder
Fuel/ignition system	6 Weber carburetors, Bendix pump, 2 coils and distributors
Lubrication	Wet sump
Gearbox	Lamborghini 5-speed
Transmission	Rear-wheel drive
Clutch	Dry single-plate, hydraulically assisted
Dry weight	1480 kg
Top speed	152 mph

OPPOSITE: Essentially an iteration of the 350 GT and 400 GT line, the conservatively styled Islero was Ferruccio's idea of what the company should be making for men like him. He proudly took one as his daily transport, but customers were less enthusiastic.

By contrast, the Islero, seen by Ferruccio as the ultimate in GT luxury, was thoroughly overshadowed when it made its debut alongside the Espada at the 1968 Geneva show. Visitors immediately identified it as another iteration of the 350 GT and 400 GT theme, and a rather bland one at that. For all the drama implied by its name (Islero was a Miura bull that fatally gored the famous Spanish bullfighter Manolete in 1947), outwardly the new car was discretion personified. Patrick McNally—the *Autosport* grand prix reporter who drove a Ferrari to work and would later run Formula 1's lucrative Paddock Club—harrumphed that the Islero had "little to recommend it" over the 400 GT 2+2 other than providing more headroom for the rear passengers.

Formerly of Carrozzeria Touring, co-designer Federico Formenti had previously worked on the Ferrari 166MM and the Alfa Romeo Disco Volante, as well as the 400 GT-based Flying Star II show car, which was among Touring's last works. That the Islero was a much more restrained piece of automotive sculpture owes much to the influence of Ferruccio Lamborghini himself, since he saw the Islero and its predecessors as the kind of GTs for which men such as himself—mature and eschewing ostentation—were the target market. He was so impressed with the Islero that he took one as his daily driver.

As with the final 400 GTs, Carrozzeria Marazzi took on the construction, and the Islero had much in common with its predecessor, being based around fundamentally the same chassis design with just a few tweaks to the suspension geometry. As a new company formed by refugees from Touring's collapse, Marazzi lacked the resources to manufacture the Islero to the standards expected by its target market, and early road tests contrasted the inexactitude of the fit and finish with the car's immaculate road manners. Demand only called for 125 examples in the first year, prompting Lamborghini to develop an S model in which the V-12's compression ratio and cam profiles were brought closer to that of the Miura for it to exude more character. A larger air scoop in the hood and flared wheel arches, plus gill-style air outlets behind the front wheels, added a sprinkle of visual pep, but still the Islero failed to entice buyers. Only 100 more were sold. Even today, Isleros coming up for sale command much lower prices than other Lamborghinis—but marque purists rightly view it as one of the most accomplished and desirable GTs to have emerged from Sant'Agata.

By mid-1969, disappointed by the Islero's sales but still unable to let go of the concept itself, Ferruccio directed new chief engineer Paolo Stanzani to conjure a replacement, with Marcello Gandini superintending the exterior and interior styling. Mindful of costs, Stanzani based the new design on the steel platform chassis concept of the Espada, albeit one nearly 11 inches shorter, giving the new car more squat and purposeful proportions. Gandini was directed to keep the middle-aged businessman demographic in mind and the result was suitably undramatic, save for the flip-down headlamp covers.

Islero 400 GTS

Chassis	Steel tube frame
Suspension	Independent double wishbones front/rear, coil springs, telescopic shock absorbers, anti-roll bars
Brakes	Unventilated Girling discs
Wheelbase	2550 mm
Front/rear track	1380 mm/1380 mm
Wheels/Tires	15 in × 7 in, Pirelli Cinturato 205/15
Engine	Front longitudinally mounted 60-degree V-12
Bore/Stroke	82 mm/62 mm
Cubic capacity	3939 cc
Compression ratio	10.8:1
Maximum power	350 bhp at 7700 rpm
Valve gear	Dual overhead camshafts, chain drive, 2 valves per cylinder
Fuel/ignition system	6 Weber carburetors, Bendix pump, 2 coils and distributors
Lubrication	Wet sump
Gearbox	ZF 5-speed
Transmission	Rear-wheel drive
Clutch	Dry single-plate, hydraulically assisted
Dry weight	1460 kg
Top speed	161 mph

Another stab at the respectable-middle-aged-businessman demographic, the Jarama was more restrained than other Marcello Gandini-designed Lamborghinis. More purposeful-looking than the Islero but still a little overweight, it did not sell in large numbers.

The method of construction chosen for the Jarama—Bertone manufacturing pressed-steel chassis and body panels for final assembly at Marazzi—meant the car was nearly 220 pounds heavier than the Islero, blunting performance. Launched at Geneva in 1970 to muted applause, the Jarama (named after a breed of fighting bull hailing from La Mancha) found just 177 buyers over two years before Lamborghini produced an S model featuring a cosmetically and materially improved interior, power steering, and a package of engine and exhaust modifications (which yielded another 15 brake horsepower). Build quality still failed to impress, and only 150 S models were sold.

Nevertheless, Ferruccio considered the Jarama to be among his finest works. Speaking to *Thoroughbred & Classic Car* magazine in 1991, he said, "I preferred the Jarama to all the others, because it is the perfect compromise between the Miura and the Espada. The Miura is a sports car for the young at heart who want to go like hell and love to be seen. Myself, I considered the Miura too extroverted after a while. In turn, the Espada was my Rolls-Royce: still quite fast, but also large and comfortable. The Jarama is the perfect car if you just want to have one car."

Initial development of the Islero overlapped with a more ambitious model, one which Ferruccio hoped might colonize a market then served by the Porsche 911 and the "baby Ferrari" 246 Dino. Stanzani's brief to bring the new car, to be called the Urraco ("little bull"), in at an accessible price point required compromise, not least since it was to be powered by a new small-displacement V-8. By adopting more contemporary design ideas than the V-12, including Heron cylinder heads (which were simpler to machine and therefore cheaper, and permitted less complex valve gear)

and belt drive rather than chains for the single overhead camshafts, Stanzani hoped it would be cheaper to make. Aluminum alloy construction throughout made the 2.5-liter unit competitively light, though it was not as powerful as it might be because of the less racy cylinder head design. But this would at least make it easier to comply with increasingly stringent US emissions regulations.

MacPherson strut suspension also reduced costs and was more space efficient than a double-wishbone arrangement, enabling the Urraco to boast more interior space—although you would struggle to convince occupants of the "+2" seats of this. Stanzani cut overhead costs elsewhere by buying in parts from other manufacturers. The front suspension uprights, for instance, were shared with the Fiat 130 saloon, the brake calipers with BMW's 2002, and the clutch was from the Mercedes parts bin. Bob Wallace industriously fettled this unpromising-sounding confection into a package that drove and felt as a Lamborghini should, aided by the mid-mounted V-8's transverse alignment.

When the Urraco was launched at the Turin show in November 1970, the Gandini-designed bodyshell attracted widespread praise and a seemingly healthy order book. But the car was nowhere near finished and ready for production. As detailed in the Countach chapter, developing the Urraco alongside a new supercar proved too resource-intensive as the Lamborghini empire's circumstances changed. The new V-8's cooling architecture and belt-driven timing gear proved especially troublesome. It took another two years for the first Urraco to be delivered, during which time many putative buyers had given up and cancelled—and Ferruccio himself was looking to cash out.

Jarama GT400

Chassis	Steel semi-monocoque
Suspension	Independent double wishbones front/rear, coil springs, telescopic shock absorbers, anti-roll bars
Brakes	Ventilated Girling discs
Wheelbase	2380 mm
Front/rear track	1490 mm/1490 mm
Wheels/Tires	15 in × 7 in, Pirelli Cinturato or Michelin XWX 215/15 (front) 225/70 (rear)
Engine	Rear transverse-mounted 60-degree V-12
Bore/Stroke	82 mm/62 mm
Cubic capacity	3939 cc
Compression ratio	10.7:1
Maximum power	350 bhp at 7500 rpm
Valve gear	Dual overhead camshafts, chain drive, 2 valves per cylinder
Fuel/ignition system	6 Weber carburetors, Bendix pump, 2 coils and distributors
Lubrication	Wet sump
Gearbox	Lamborghini 5-speed manual TorqueFlite 3-speed automatic
Transmission	Rear-wheel drive
Clutch	Dry single-plate, hydraulically assisted
Dry weight	1450 kg
Top speed	161 mph

Urraco

Chassis	Steel platform
Suspension	Independent MacPherson front/rear, coil springs, telescopic shock absorbers
Brakes	Ventilated Girling discs
Wheelbase	2450 mm
Front/rear track	1460 mm/1460 mm
Wheels/Tires	14 in × 7.5 in, Michelin XWX 195/14 (front) 205/14 (rear)
Engine	Mid-mounted 90-degree V-8
Bore/Stroke	77.4 mm/53 mm (P200) 88 mm/53 mm (P250) 86 mm/64.5 mm (P300)
Cubic capacity	1994 cc (P200), 2463 cc (P250), 2996 cc (P300)
Compression ratio	8.6:1 (P200), 10.5:1 (P250, P300)
Maximum power	182 bhp at 7500 rpm (P200) 220 bhp at 7500 rpm (P250) 250 bhp at 7500 rpm (P300)
Valve gear	Overhead camshafts, belt drive, 2 valves per cylinder; double overhead camshafts, chain drive, 2 valves per cylinder (P300)
Fuel/ignition system	4 Weber carburetors, Bendix pump, 1 coil and distributor
Lubrication	Wet sump
Gearbox	Lamborghini 5-speed
Transmission	Rear-wheel drive
Clutch	Dry single-plate, hydraulically assisted
Dry weight	1100 kg
Top speed	134 mph (P200), 149 mph (P250), 161 mph (P300)

On the road, the Urraco was brisk rather than quick. At Turin in 1974, Lamborghini introduced the P300 model, the car the original P250 arguably ought to have been, featuring a more opulently trimmed interior and an enlarged 3-liter version of the V-8 with twin chain-driven camshafts. Despite its qualities, the P300 was outshone by the new Ferrari 308 Dino, and ultimately only 205 were sold. The Italy-only P200 model, built around a downsized engine to circumvent Italian taxation rules, also failed to set the market alight. Despite great hopes for the US market, an adapted version of the P250 with the obligatory safety bumpers and a detuned engine (to meet emissions regulations) found just 21 customers. Americans with a desire for a European sports-car preferred the private import route.

The Urraco was aimed at the Porsche 911 and the Ferrari 246 Dino. Though it didn't match their sales, it is now coveted by brand aficionados.

COUNTACH

"COUNTACH!" THIS EARTHY PIECE OF PIEDMONTESE VERNACULAR—for which there is no exact translation, but it was typically used by young men in appreciation of an attractive lady—has been variously attributed to Nuccio Bertone and Ferruccio Lamborghini as they first clapped eyes on the prototype then known as Project 112. Since Lamborghini was born and brought up in Emilia-Romagna, it's more plausible to imagine that it was Bertone, a Piedmontese through and through, who was moved to ejaculate thus as he appraised Marcello Gandini's wedgy work-in-progress.

SUPERCAR POSTER BOY

By 1969 Lamborghini appeared to be ticking over nicely as a car manufacturer, with its flagship model now as mechanically sorted as it could be (in the form of the Miura S), and the four-seater Espada finding customers. But the first rumblings of the troubles that would engulf the company could be felt. Ferruccio's ambitions to offer a broad model range were thwarted by inconsistent quality control and lack of demand for the humbler models, such as the unloved Islero, a follow-up to the 400GT, which sold only 225 examples from 1968 to 1970. New models were in the pipeline, including the front-engined Jarama—a replacement for the Islero with more adventurous styling—and the Urraco, which was to have a 2.5-liter V-8 engine and function as a kind of junior Miura. Unfortunately, the Jarama was destined never to catch on and the Urraco would suffer endless development delays, finally entering production in 1973, three years after its Turin show debut.

Lamborghini needed volume to grow as a manufacturer, yet its production arrangements were still scattershot, with small-scale coachbuilders such as Marazzi building the bodies of cars such as the Islero and Jarama, but struggling to get the quality right. And there were philosophical problems for the Miura, which by rights ought to be the more exclusive "halo" model, and yet was selling in too great a quantity for it to be truly rarefied. Another practical concern was the emergence of rivals from just down the road, and not only from Maranello: to the Ferrari 365 GTB/4 "Daytona" add the Maserati Bora and De Tomaso Mangusta.

So in 1970 Lamborghini's engineers set to work on a successor to the Miura. "Project 112" would be an altogether different car; faster, visually more dramatic, and more technically advanced. Ferruccio had never quite reconciled himself to the presence of a screaming V-12 just behind his head, and his desire for greater separation between the occupants and the reciprocating masses of the engine is one of the reasons given for relocating the engine from a transverse position to a longitudinal one. This, together with an enlargement of the V-12 to five liters, would lead to the

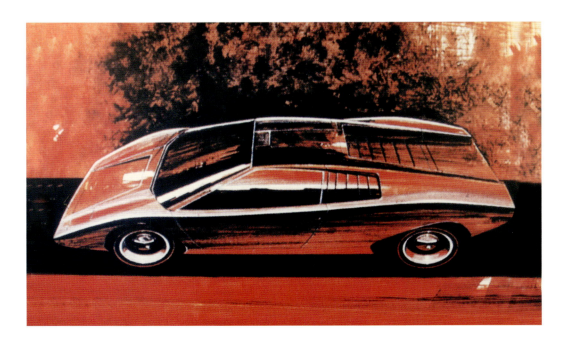

Gandini's early sketches of the LP500 show a beautiful purity of line that had to be compromised in places as manufacturing reality got in the way of idealistic vision.

car being rechristened LP500 (LP for Longitudinale Posteriore, meaning the engine's alignment and rearward positioning) before ultimately becoming the Countach.

Some years later Peter Coltrin, an expatriate American journalist and photographer who was privy to the car's development, would describe Lamborghini's manifesto in *The Motor* magazine:

> It would be a true "macchina sportive stradale"—neither a GT car nor a race car but a car guaranteed to do, among other things, a standing kilometer in 23 seconds or less. It would combine performance with comfort. Performance here was defined as a high power-to-weight ratio, stability and maneuverability. None of these qualities could be neglected, each had to have a well-thought-out approach and solution. The car would not be built to a price. As far as was practicable, cost would be no object to achieve the aims although, as with all things, the line has finally to be drawn somewhere. The car would be sold only to discerning customers, known to the factory—serious enthusiasts who would appreciate the car and know how to use it. A prestige car by its very nature, but not for "status symbol" seekers. Too many of the latter gave the Miura a somewhat tarnished reputation—like pop stars who made headlines by crashing as many as three Miuras and others whose line of "business" didn't exactly enhance the Miura's image.

In this you can see the beginnings of a line of thought that the company remains faithful to today.

Ferruccio again directed his engineers—now led by Paolo Stanzani following the departure of Gian Paolo Dallara—to work closely with Bertone, who would be responsible for the design and build of the bodyshell. The experience of trying to tame the Miura's unruly on-the-limit behavior was as prominent in Stanzani's mind as the need for better insulation from engine noise, and this informed the decision to move to a spaceframe chassis with the engine located on a north-south axis within it. The V-12's new location would make it easier to cool, yield a more optimal exhaust layout, and give better weight distribution—provided it could be packaged within the wheelbase.

This provided a challenge since V-12s are intrinsically quite long, and with a transmission in the conventional place—aft of the engine—some of the drivetrain's mass would end up behind the rear axle line. Stanzani's clever solution was to turn the whole system around so that the engine's power was output forward to a clutch and gearbox located between the hips of the driver and passenger. As well as improving the car's polar moment of inertia, this gave a more direct connection to the gear linkage (although owners would still require the quads of a power lifter to work the clutch). The disadvantages came in the form of introducing a different form of mechanical noise to the cabin, and a more complex system of transferring motive force from the gearbox to the rear axle, via a shaft through the sump.

At Bertone's studios, Marcello Gandini had already produced one stunning wedge-shaped vehicle, the Stratos Zero, as part of a stealth pitch to Lancia. It had been unveiled, to popular acclaim, at the Turin show in 1970, though some features—such as the large glass windscreen that hinged upward to furnish access to the cabin—were clearly not practical for a series production car. Mercedes had already produced a sports car with gull-wing doors in the 1950s. For the LP500, Gandini began his sketch of the side elevation with a single sweeping, unbroken line from nose to tail; this would dictate the path of every other line, as well as the glasshouse and the proportions of the flanks—and the shape of the doors. For these, Gandini proposed something that had never been seen on a production car: hinging upwards from the front so that they opened like scissors.

Countless show-goers at Geneva in March 1971 expressed sentiments along the lines of *countach!* when they clocked the LP500 prototype, even though many harbored doubts that it could become a workable production car. There were those who believed Lamborghini was simply showing off, and if the exterior wasn't outlandish enough to promote such a notion, then the peculiarly half-finished cabin—with its all-electronic instruments and what looked like the control yoke of an aircraft rather than a steering wheel—was enough to tip some over the edge.

Nevertheless, with the LP500 lining up on the stand alongside the new Miura SV, a revised Espada, the Urraco, and Jarama, Lamborghini seemed a picture of health. The truth was rather different. Even as putative customers lined up to indicate that they'd take an LP500 if Lamborghini built it, pressure was mounting both within and without.

The engineering and development team was stretched too thinly to deliver the Urraco and LP500 to production in the necessary timeframe, and it quickly became apparent that the LP500, in its transition to becoming the Countach, had to be substantially reengineered. This would require substantial investment, just at the time Ferruccio Lamborghini's industrial interests were coming under pressure from the slowing global economy and the beginnings of the energy crisis (oil production in the United States had already peaked when the wraps came off the LP500 at Geneva, and was beginning to decline).

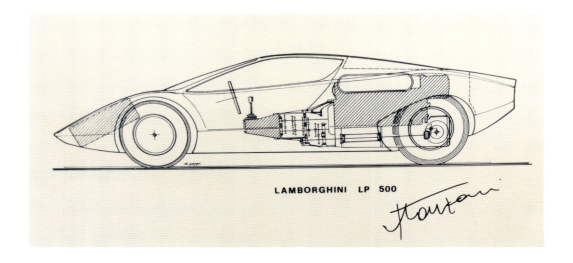

To centralize the weight of the Countach as much as possible, Paolo Stanzani reengineered the transmission to sit ahead of the engine, with the drive output shaft running through the sump.

Lamborghini's tractor business, the one that had provided the launching point for everything else, was among the first to be hit by declining domestic and international sales—at a time when the company had invested heavily after landing a major order from the socialist government led by Juan José Torres in Bolivia. Then, in a twin blow, the South African importer canceled its orders, while the hundreds of tractors destined for Bolivia were never shipped after Torres was overthrown (with the clandestine backing, some believe, of the Nixon administration in the USA) in a coup d'état led by General Hugo Banzer Suárez. Lamborghini was trapped with a vast quantity of unsold inventory.

Automobili Lamborghini also faced declining sales as customers held on for the Urraco and Countach—cars whose development was stalling for lack of investment. First to feel the pinch was the five-liter version of the V-12. Ongoing difficulties with the Urraco V-8 sucked time and resources, and there wasn't enough money in the pot to make the reworked V-12 reliable enough. But Stanzani was able to redevelop the Countach's spaceframe chassis from its initial iteration as a network of square tubes. The new chassis used thinner round-section tubes, rather like the classic Superleggera designs pioneered by Carrozzeria Touring.

As Bob Wallace clocked up the testing miles on the roads around Sant'Agata and at the Varano circuit to the north, it became clear that the radiators were not receiving enough air from the louvers on the car's "shoulders" to cope with the engine's thermal demands. Stanzani and fellow engineer Massimo Parenti conducted ride-alongs in an effort to understand the Countach's aerodynamics, taking motor-drive photos of it at speed after gluing wool tufts to its flanks, and noting the temperature characteristics with a Telemax gauge.

The LP500 prototype was extraordinarily futuristic; many visitors to the 1971 Geneva show did not believe it would be built.

Faced with declining sales and unsold stock, the obvious solution would have been for Ferruccio to lay off staff and cut production. But the deals he'd cut with the local government committed him to full unionization, and the unions wouldn't budge. Creditors, also squeezed by recession, began to line up.

As a successful entrepreneur, Ferruccio could duck and dive with the best of them, but this bull had felt more than one touch of the *espada*. He kept most of the creditors at arm's length by reaching cash settlements, but these depleted his resources further. By the end of 1971 it was becoming clear to him that if he wanted to enjoy a comfortable retirement and preserve the Lamborghini legacy for his son Tonino, he would have to cut his exposure to risk, let go of the underperforming businesses, and shore up his personal finances.

In 1972 Ferruccio agreed to sell a 51-percent shareholding in Automobili Lamborghini to one of his customers, Georges-Henri Rossetti. The Swiss, a scion of a wealthy family with business interests in—among other things—watch manufacture, Rossetti was what we would now call a "car guy," a serial owner of sports cars and a sometime Formula 3 racer in his youth. The amount that changed hands was reported to be $600,000.

Ferruccio offloaded the tractor business entirely to one of its main rivals, the Italian S.A.M.E group, for an undisclosed sum, but while he was now a minority shareholder in Automobili Lamborghini he remained a more hands-on presence than Rossetti, who largely governed from afar. In May 1972 Stanzani and Wallace drove the working prototype Countach to Sicily and back to watch the Targa Florio road race, presented the unbroken car to Ferruccio and Rossetti upon their return, and were rewarded with the decision to put the car into production.

Lamborghini demonstrated a second show car version of the Countach, badged LP400 in deference to its use of the existing V-12, at the 1973 Geneva show, but it would not be production-ready until a year later. Some of the purity of Gandini's original design had to be compromised for the sake of engine cooling, so by launch the Countach grew two features that would become distinctive signatures: NACA ducts on each side and boxy air intakes on the shoulders. There were detail changes, too, around the side windows, although they could still not be fully opened. The orange Countach shown in this chapter is one of just 150 to have been built with Gandini's periscope-style rearview mirror, and a similar example fetched $1,210,000 at auction in 2014.

By launch time, Ferruccio had sold the remaining shareholding in Automobili Lamborghini to another Swiss, Rene Leimer, for $400,000 and retired to his Umbrian estate, leaving the remaining businesses in the hands of Tonino. In the three-year gap between show car model and Countach launch, world economies had crashed and gasoline prices had gone through the roof as a result, largely, of conflict in the Middle East. Several countries, including Italy, placed punitive taxes on "gas guzzlers," prompting Lamborghini's new owners to go so far as offering a two-liter version of the Urraco. It was received with little interest.

The yellow Countach prototype is the closest to Gandini's original vision. The production car would gain an NACA duct on each side and bulkier, less elegant air intakes.
Giles Chapman Library

Countach LP400

Chassis	Steel spaceframe
Suspension	Independent double wishbones, coil springs and telescopic shock absorbers, anti-roll bar (front); independent lower double wishbones with upper transverse links and radius arms, twin coil springs and telescopic shock absorbers, anti-roll bar (rear)
Brakes	Ventilated Girling discs
Wheelbase	2450 mm
Front/rear track	1500 mm/1520 mm
Wheels/Tires	14 in × 7.5 in, Michelin XWX 205/70 (front); 14 in × 9.5 in, Michelin XWX 215/70 (rear)
Engine	Rear longitudinal-mounted 60-degree V-12
Bore/Stroke	82 mm/62 mm
Cubic capacity	3929 cc
Compression ratio	10.5:1
Maximum power	375 bhp at 8000 rpm (claimed)
Valve gear	Dual overhead camshafts, chain drive, 2 valves per cylinder
Fuel/ignition system	Dual Bendix pumps, 6 Weber DCOE carburettors, 2 coils
Lubrication	Wet sump
Gearbox	Lamborghini 5-speed manual
Transmission	Two-wheel drive
Clutch	Dry single-plate
Dry weight	1055 kg
Top speed	196 mph (claimed)

The Countach therefore appeared irrelevant, and it is in this context that we must view some of the press coverage of the time. When *Motor* magazine obtained an LP400 to road test late in 1975, it resulted in the peculiar juxtaposition of a cover photo featuring the car smoking away from the standing start (with a Peiseler "fifth wheel" performance-measuring device hanging off the back) and an editorial that didn't mince words: "Is it the fastest production car in the world? Maybe. The best car in the world? No. But what Lamborghini's Countach does have is charisma, that almost undefinable something that has children falling over its steeply raked nose and adults clamouring to squeeze into its cramped interior. But what else is in its favor? Is it even practical? Like the [Ferrari] Boxer we see this former Geneva show-stopper as one of a dying breed and it is certainly not as useful a device as Lamborghini's own Urraco—itself not quite in the mould of Lotus's 'power with economy' offerings."

One can almost imagine the editor, having composed this rumination, pausing to refill his pipe with Old Holborn and taking a meditative puff. A workmanlike fixation with practicality, which to modern eyes reads akin to a failure of joy and imagination, pervades this and the road test to which it was attached: "Few people gazing at the original Bertone Countach at Geneva in 1971 could have regarded it as anything other than a 'show' car. There were those fold-up doors for a start (how did you get out if the car rolled?) and the space-age cockpit with its abysmal rear visibility . . . it seemed unlikely."

Still, this was published in a Britain where commercial use of electricity had recently been rationed to three days a week, and the motoring press remained parochial apologists for a declining domestic industry, so the authors should perhaps be forgiven for allocating space in the first proper independent performance test of the Countach to mere matters of practicality. On the whole, they rather liked the car, even though it

cost more than a small house and did not meet the claimed performance figures—which they generously attributed to the engine not being properly run-in.

Wholesale change tends to make human beings feel uncomfortable and insecure, and so it was with the factory workforce at Automobili Lamborghini. Some of the more hagiographic accounts of the company's history dwell on Ferruccio's man-of-the-people credentials, and while he was indeed more hands-on than his successors it is unlikely that he spent quite as much time on the factory floor as some authors suggest. The schism between management and workers began as a consequence of the faltering economy before Ferruccio's retirement, and if it widened afterward it was not so much a factor of the new owners' management style as the fact that they were foreigners.

Nor were Leimer and Rossetti able to wrestle with all the financial problems that faced the company. The Urraco was a sales bomb, and the Countach took too long to build (just 23 left the factory in 1974) to satisfy demand, largely because the frame was outsourced to Marchesi and then hand-finished at Sant'Agata, while many minor components that would normally be brought in from outside were expensively hand-made in-house. Stanzani and Wallace left in 1975, feeling that there would be no new car in the pipeline to get their teeth into, and the new owners hired Gian Paolo Dallara as a consultant to steer development.

On Dallara's watch, Lamborghini produced two special Countachs for private customers—an Italian collector and Canadian Formula 1 team owner Walter Wolf—that would pave the way for the next evolution of the production model. He added a front air dam and rear wing, along with fiberglass wheelarch extensions to accommodate the biggest mechanical change, larger rear wheels. The Michelin XWX boots the LP400 rode on were the largest available at the time, but the 14-inch wheel size these imposed limited the car's braking capacity as well as its road-holding. Pirelli's new PZero enabled Dallara to fit 15-inch wheels and larger brake rotors, and the lower profile of the new tire made for less sidewall squidge under duress.

These, along with some interior changes, fed in to the 1978 Countach LP400S, along with the removal of the periscope mirror and roof groove, and a rather more accurate claim for the V-12's power (353 brake horsepower). But the company was still in trouble; Rossetti rarely visited the factory, and Leimer struggled to manage the competing demands for his time from his own companies and Lamborghini. The strain on Sant'Agata's finances and engineering resources grew when new European Union legislation demanded that all cars offered for sale from 1978 onward had to meet more stringent crash-test regulations in order to gain a type-approval certificate. This killed all but one of Lamborghini's model range at a stroke and resulted in a modest weight gain for the Countach, which had to be offered with the rear spoiler as an optional extra since it would not pass type approval as standard equipment.

At the same time, Lamborghini signed up to two potentially lucrative outside partnerships that would prove catastrophic. It undertook to manufacture BMW's new Giugiaro-styled performance car, the M1, and develop an off-road vehicle codenamed Cheetah for an American company, with a view to obtaining military contracts. These were enough to secure a loan from the Italian government, but both projects would founder; persistent industrial unrest meant very few M1s were built and BMW soon looked elsewhere, while the Cheetah became entangled in an intellectual property dispute between Lamborghini's American client and the Ford Motor Company.

In desperation, Leimer raised a loan from US businessman Zoltan Reti, secured on the factory. Within months Reti wanted his money back and had the company declared bankrupt. As the receivers moved in, Rossetti and Leimer became merely unsecured creditors, ultimately receiving nothing from the company's sale. Lamborghini was lucky that the appointed receiver, Dr. Alexandro Artese, was a car nut who felt it was worth saving rather than breaking up to appease the secured creditors. He recruited Giulio Alfieri, formerly of Maserati, to run the factory and act as chief engineer, and production of the Countach continued.

Only one set of serious buyers for the company came forward, and in January 1981 the assets of Automobili Lamborghini changed hands for $3 million. The new owners, Patrick and Jean-Claude Mimran, were scions of a Franco-Swiss family that had substantial mining and sugar-production interests in Senegal. They set up a new

company, Nuova Automobili Ferruccio Lamborghini SpA, of which 24-year-old Patrick was the president.

Just two months later, the company appeared at the Geneva show with a prototype Alfieri had been developing as an Urraco replacement—the Jalpa, a putative new Miura styled by a Swiss company—and an early version of a pseudo-military off-roader based on the moribund Cheetah. The Mimrans also pushed forward with plans to develop the Countach, and Alfieri oversaw the biggest change the model had seen in a decade.

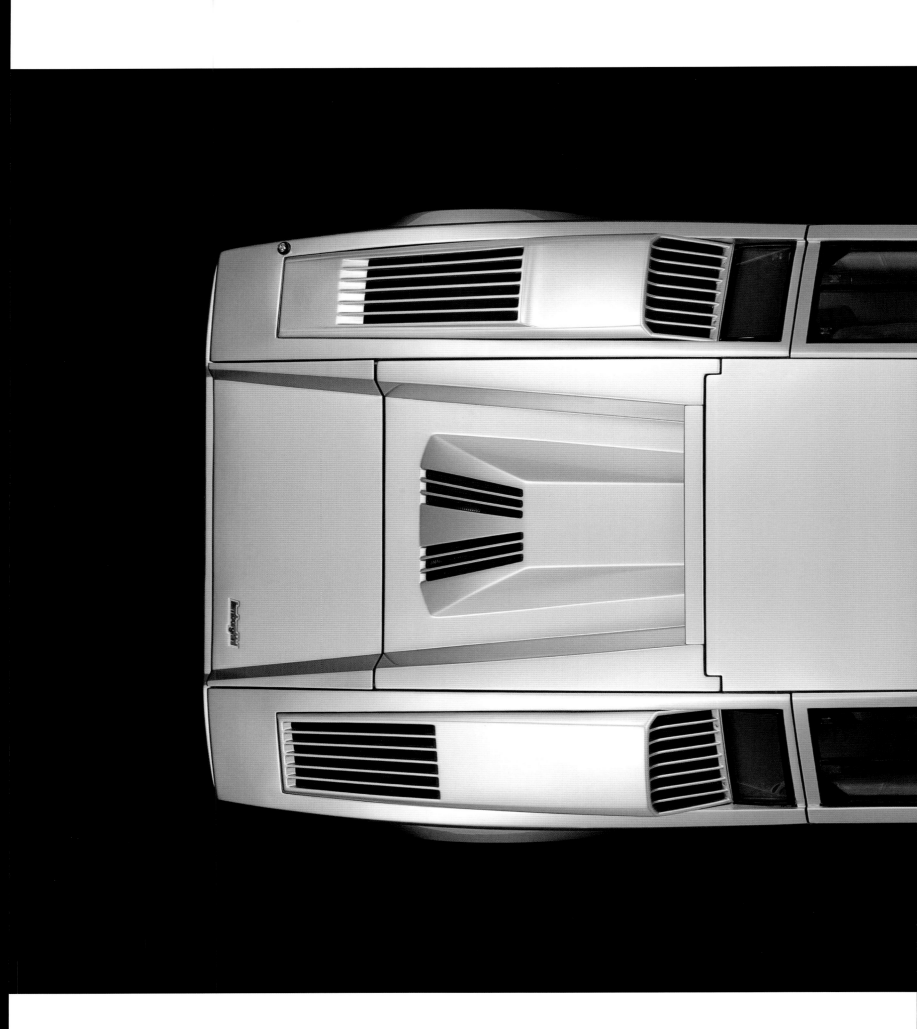

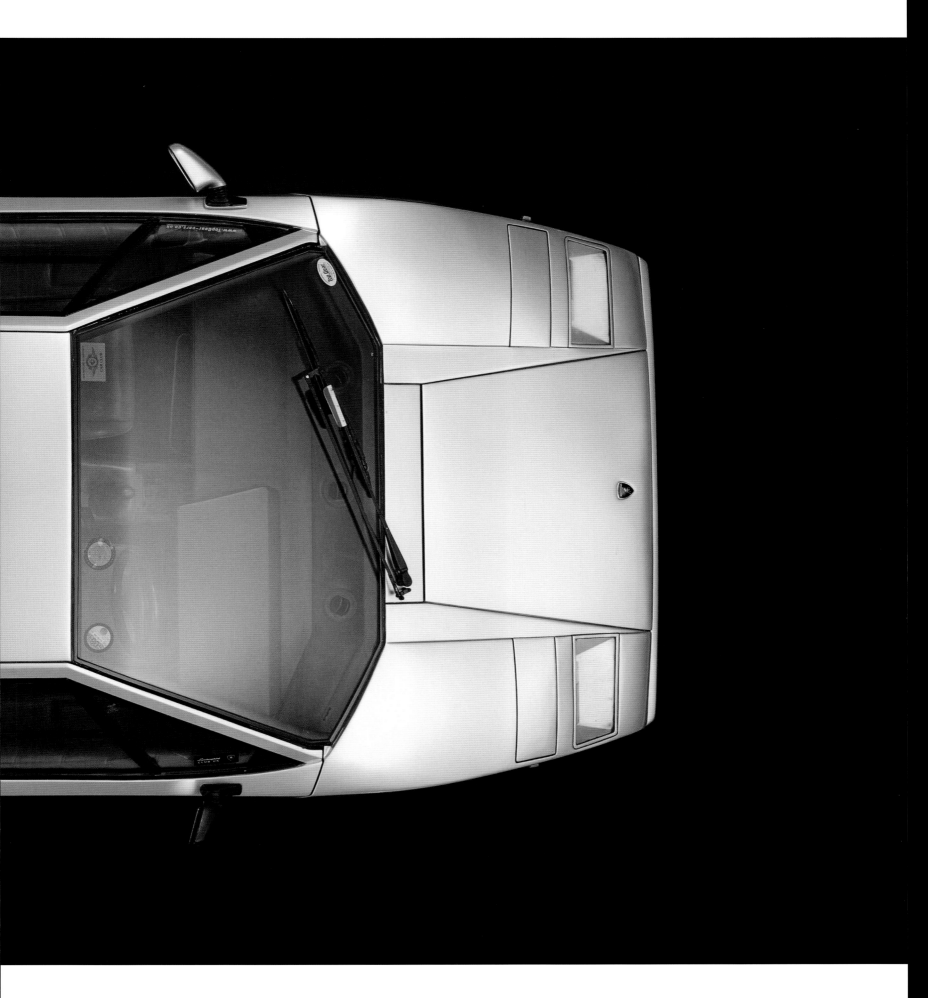

Countach 25th Anniversary

Based on the LP5000 Quattrovalvole, the Countach 25th Anniversary model introduced in 1988 to celebrate the company's quarter-century featured redesigned spoilers, skirts, rear lights and intake vents.

Keeping in touch with newer rivals such as Ferrari was a difficult proposition because the Countach's distinctive shape was far less streamlined than it looked, particularly with fatter wheelarches and a large rear wing. The obvious tactic would be to unleash more horses. Together with new recruit Luigi Marmiroli, Alfieri expanded the engine to just short of five liters (4,754 cc), enabling the new LP500S model to achieve a real-world top speed of around 180 miles per hour. They improved the interior accommodations too, by raising the roof 1.2 inches.

In the wider world, the Countach rose the conspicuous-consumption zeitgeist of the 1980s. Incredibly, in a fast-forward decade where the fashions, chattels, and philosophies of previous eras were declared axiomatically ungood, a car designed in the early 1970s continued to be the defining object of automotive lust. Posters featuring it took pride of place on the bedroom walls of billions of teenagers.

The Countach moved with the bubble-permed times by becoming ever more dramatic: bigger wheels, bigger arches, bigger wings. Yet more power was required to push this increasingly muscular piece of road-going real estate through the air, and because of limited space in the engine compartment, turbocharging wasn't an option. The engine itself would have to grow.

Marmiroli and Alfieri had been working on a seven-liter development of the V-12 for use in the military off-roader and fed some of the lessons into one that could be shoehorned into the Countach. Keeping the same bore as the existing unit but expanding the stroke from 69 to 75 mm gave a swept volume of 5,167 cc, and this, along with new heads featuring four valves per cylinder, gave a more even power curve, which peaked at between 455 and 470 brake horsepower.

The 5000 Quattrovalvole appeared in 1985, sporting several Kevlar panels to offset the increasing bulk, and with a bulging engine cover that made the contents of the rearview mirror even more academic. The question now was: Could the car attain the 200 miles per hour that had been claimed back in Geneva, 1971?

In a story for *Fast Lane* magazine in 1986, noted writer Peter Dron described a stealth drive on an *autostrada* with Pierluigi Martini (soon to become a Formula 1 driver and Le Mans winner) where he used kilometer markers to calculate the QV's top speed: "Martini talks of regularly having seen 320kmh (roughly one digit short of 200mph) on his speedometer, even at night. The pop-up headlights, he claims, make very little difference to the drag factor. Once, he says, the reading was 325kmh.

"This is the sort of wild, fanciful stuff we have heard about the QV5000S for some time. Frankly it is hard to believe, but if we can find a break in the traffic, we'll put it to the test."

That they duly did. He continued:

> In our ignorance of the Countach, we not only disbelieved the performance claims for it, but we also believed that myth about the car being unstable at high speed without the wing fitted. That may have been true of the earlier version, but it certainly doesn't apply to the Quattrovalvole which runs arrow-straight at its maximum speed. . . .
>
> We try again and again, but each time we are baulked as the inevitable man in a little Fiat pulls out to pass a truck, all the while almost facing his lady passenger. . . . Finally, we turn off on to a different autostrada. It's clear, and the rev needle is flickering wildly just inside the red sector, and the speedometer is reading 320kmh. This is it.
>
> We pass the first kilometer post. Those tiny specks in the far distance are beginning to be identifiable shapes. Soon, though they would not be aware of it even if they used their rear-view mirrors, they could become a braking area. Click! We pass the second kilometer post and Piero is safely, very firmly on the brakes. We've covered a flying kilometer in 11.46sec, which is 314.1kmh metric, 195.2mph imperial, and bloody quick in anyone's language. Countach!

GIULIO ALFIERI

An engineer with impeccable pedigree, Giulio Alfieri joined Lamborghini in 1978 as he began the glide path toward retirement, but his work at Sant'Agata was no less notable than it had been over the preceding three decades. Born in Parma in 1924, he studied engineering in Milan, graduating during the turmoil of the postwar years.

After initially finding work building steam turbines for nautical use, Alfieri joined Innocenti, maker of the iconic Lambretta scooters, in 1949. Four years later he moved to Modena to work alongside the likes of Gioacchino Colombo at Maserati. It was a chaotic time, since the company was developing its promising and potentially lucrative 250F Formula 1 car at the same time that owner Adolfo Orsi juggled the finances to stay afloat. Alfieri was involved in the design of the 250F's 2.5-liter straight-six engine and would work on a string of other iconic Maserati projects, including a V-12 engine (which ultimately saw service in Formula 1 in the late 1960s) and the beautiful lightweight Tipo 1 "Birdcage."

Alfieri remained at Maserati through financially turbulent times. Orsi's supposedly lucrative contract to supply machine tools to Argentina brought the company to the brink of ruin, as a similar deal with South America would cripple Lamborghini two decades later: Argentine dictator General Peron was toppled in a coup d'état and his successors never paid the bill. This left Maserati owing Italian banks a fortune, and by 1958 Credito Italiano was calling for Orsi's head. The company stumbled on until it was acquired by French automaker Citroen, first as a minority shareholder in 1967 and then outright in 1971.

Alfieri enjoyed another fruitful period, overseeing the Maserati Merak, Khamsin, and Bora as well as a V-6 engine in two displacements for Citroen's flagship sports saloon, the futuristic SM. But the relationship was not to last. The oil crisis of the early 1970s killed sales of gas-guzzling machinery, and Maserati's production was hit by the same kind of industrial unrest that bedeviled Lamborghini. Citroen's bean counters cried "enough" in 1975, declared the company bankrupt, and made the workforce redundant.

Maserati existed in limbo again, bankrolled by a government-backed holding company and a new minority shareholder, the colorful character Alejandro De Tomaso, who proposed a ruthless medicine: cutting around 50 percent of the workforce. Alfieri was among that number, reputedly finding the contents of his office waiting for him in the car park as he arrived for work.

At Lamborghini, Alfieri found himself in a classic out-of-the-frying-pan-into-the-fire scenario until new investment from the Mimran brothers gave the company sufficient financial security to invest in the model range. As technical director, Alfieri developed the new Jalpa model and oversaw the Countach's rebirth as a 1980s icon, eventually retiring after the Chrysler takeover in 1987. He passed away in 2002, shortly before his 78th birthday, after a short illness.

Countach Quattrovalvole / Anniversary

Chassis	Steel spaceframe
Suspension	Independent double wishbones, coil springs and telescopic shock absorbers, anti-roll bar (front); independent lower double wishbones with upper transverse links and radius arms, twin coil springs and telescopic shock absorbers, anti-roll bar (rear)
Brakes	Ventilated ATE discs
Wheelbase	2500 mm
Front/rear track	1536 mm/1606 mm
Wheels/Tires	15 in × 8.5 in, Pirelli P7F 225/50 (front); 16 in × 12 in, Pirelli P7F 345/45 (rear)
Anniversary	15 in × 8.5 in, Pirelli PZero 225/50 (front); 16 in × 12 in, Pirelli PZero 345/35 (rear)
Engine	Rear longitudinal-mounted 60-degree V-12
Bore/Stroke	85.5 mm/75 mm
Cubic capacity	5167 cc
Compression ratio	9.5:1
Maximum power	455 bhp at 7000 rpm (claimed)
Valve gear	Dual overhead camshafts, chain drive, 4 valves per cylinder
Fuel/ignition system	Dual Bendix pumps, 6 Weber DCNF carburettors, electronic ignition
Lubrication	Wet sump
Gearbox	Lamborghini 5-speed manual
Transmission	Two-wheel drive
Clutch	Dry single-plate
Dry weight	1490 kg
Top speed	184 mph (claimed)

Six hundred and thirty-one units of the QV5000S would be built. Lamborghini was on a high in 1986 as the Mimrans entered negotiations to sell the company to Chrysler. The 200-miles-per-hour barrier still beckoned, and during 1987 Alfieri worked on a mobile test bed known as the Evoluzione, which featured a racing-style aluminum monocoque and aluminum panels.

Though scoop photos led many to believe this was a new Countach model, it was little more than an engineering exercise, and the sole example built was destroyed in a crash test. The Mimrans sold out to Chrysler in May 1987 for $33 million, a handsome profit, and the company's first act under new ownership was to titivate its flagship model.

The Countach Anniversary, unveiled in 1988, celebrated a remarkable quarter century since Lamborghini's founding. Some of the bodywork additions (by Horacio Pagani) proved controversial among Lamborghini purists, but the greater use of carbon fiber prefigured Lamborghini models to come. As the silver example shown in this chapter demonstrates, the instant signifiers of the Anniversary are the straked rear shoulder airboxes, along with a larger rear bumper to satisfy US safety regulations. Those who bought the car to drive rather than tuck away as an investment found more pleasantly appointed, electrically adjustable seats in the cabin.

This latter element was seen as a mark of increasing US input into the development process. What, the world wondered, would the successor to the Countach look like now that Lamborghini was in American hands?

Countach LP400 S

Chassis	Steel spaceframe
Suspension	Independent double wishbones, coil springs and telescopic shock absorbers, anti-roll bar (front); independent lower double wishbones with upper transverse links and radius arms, twin coil springs and telescopic shock absorbers, anti-roll bar (rear)
Brakes	Ventilated Girling discs
Wheelbase	2450 mm
Front/rear track	1492 mm/1606 mm
Wheels/Tires	15 in × 8.5 in, Pirelli P7 205/50 (front); 15 in × 12 in, Pirelli P7 345/55 (rear)
Engine	Rear longitudinal-mounted 60-degree V-12
Bore/Stroke	82 mm/62 mm
Cubic capacity	3929 cc
Compression ratio	10.5:1
Maximum power	353 bhp at 7500 rpm (claimed)
Valve gear	Dual overhead camshafts, chain drive, 2 valves per cylinder
Fuel/ignition system	Dual Bendix pumps, 6 Weber DCOE carburettors, 2 coils
Lubrication	Wet sump
Gearbox	Lamborghini 5-speed manual
Transmission	Two-wheel drive
Clutch	Dry single-plate
Dry weight	1200 kg
Top speed	177 mph (claimed)

Countach LP500 S

Chassis	Steel spaceframe
Suspension	Independent double wishbones, coil springs and telescopic shock absorbers, anti-roll bar (front); independent lower double wishbones with upper transverse links and radius arms, twin coil springs and telescopic shock absorbers, anti-roll bar (rear)
Brakes	Ventilated ATE discs
Wheelbase	2450 mm
Front/rear track	1492 mm/1606 mm
Wheels/Tires	15 in × 8.5 in, Pirelli P7 205/50 (front); 15 in × 12 in, Pirelli P7 345/55 (rear)
Engine	Rear longitudinal-mounted 60-degree V-12
Bore/Stroke	85.5 mm/69 mm
Cubic capacity	4754 cc
Compression ratio	9.2:1
Maximum power	375 bhp at 7000 rpm (claimed)
Valve gear	Dual overhead camshafts, chain drive, 2 valves per cylinder
Fuel/ignition system	Dual Bendix pumps, 6 Weber DCOE carburettors, electronic ignition
Lubrication	Wet sump
Gearbox	Lamborghini 5-speed manual
Transmission	Two-wheel drive
Clutch	Dry single-plate
Dry weight	1490 kg
Top speed	186 mph (claimed)

RAISING THE ROOF

WITH THE GIFT OF HINDSIGHT, we can divine key reasons the Urraco failed to gain traction in its target market: Lamborghini's uncertain future, given the parlous and well-documented state of its finances in the mid-1970s, and the widespread perception that Lamborghinis weren't assembled to a standard concomitant with the asking price. It's perfectly understandable why, at the time, management either failed to recognize this state of affairs or felt powerless to change it. Instead, the directors turned their energies to hitherto untapped markets.

COMING TO AMERICA

Budgetary constraints meant the Silhouette was based heavily on the Urraco, but new suspension geometry enabled it to take advantage of the latest generation of Pirelli tires.

Targa-top cars presented by Porsche and Ferrari were eagerly sought after in America, a territory Lamborghini had struggled to penetrate in sufficient numbers to justify tooling up to comply with US safety and emissions regulations. Luigi Capellini, recruited to the board after Ferruccio's departure in 1974, had come from De Tomaso, which had recently introduced the Pantera to the United States with great success. Capellini quickly pushed for a new open-top model that could conquer America and ameliorate the cost of the V-8 platform.

Lamborghini once again commissioned Bertone to provide the design, using the fundamentals of the Urraco P300 as a base car to offset development costs. Shown in prototype form at the 1976 Turin Motor Show, the Silhouette would even feature the same doors and windscreen as the Urraco, although Bertone substantially reworked both the detailing and the proportions of the donor vehicle. The majority of the changes were under the skin, Gian Paulo Dallara and new chief engineer Franco Baraldini having embraced Pirelli's new low-profile P7 tire—described by Dallara as "the greatest single-component breakthrough in the history of the car." Accommodating these involved a wider track front and rear (by 34 millimeters and 62 millimeters, respectively), along with new suspension geometry and a higher final-drive ratio. Cosmetically, it permitted the fitting of Campagnolo's delightful 15-inch cast magnesium teledial wheels, which were designed specifically for the P7. To recover torsional stiffness lost through cutting a hole in the roof, Dallara beefed up the monocoque and fitted a roll-over hoop to satisfy safety regulations.

Another prerequisite for the US market was a better interior, and to this end Lamborghini adopted a new instrument binnacle with (supposedly) less scattershot location of dials and switchgear than in the Urraco. More commodious bucket seats were trimmed in plusher cloth (leather was an option), but the modifications to the chassis meant sacrificing the back row of seating to make room for stowage of the targa roof panel. The Silhouette would be a strict two-seater.

Just over a month after the Turin show, in October 1976, UK Lamborghini importer Roger Phillips arrived at Sant'Agata with two friends and *Car* magazine editor Mel Nichols to collect a Countach, an Urraco, and the first production Silhouette for exhibition at the Earl's Court show in London. Nichols would recount their 160-mile-per-hour road trip across Europe in his seminal story "Convoy," published a few months later. Not only was it a beautifully evocative high point in 1970s automotive journalism, it provided a snapshot of Lamborghini's woes: Franco Baraldini was absent, meeting BMW in Germany to usher the M1 supercar project across the line; René Leimer, also not present, was still waiting for a $1.5 million grant promised by the Italian government; and the trip was delayed by a day because the Silhouette wasn't finished, owing to strike action.

Once underway, Nichols had a few moments of magic aboard the Silhouette as the convoy negotiated the D979—"the kind of road you dream about"—through the River Ain valley in France.

"Without the car being taxed in any way, it simply devoured that road. Keeping the V8 in mid-range and just occasionally giving it its head for a moment coming out the bends brought more than enough speed; despite those curves, the speed was rarely below 70mph and frequently around 100mph. The bumps mid-bend, and they were often frightful, could not throw the Silhouette off-line. Wet patches encountered under brakes into hairpins did not make it budge an inch.

"Ah, how well it could all be felt through that leatherbound wheel and the pliant but ideally controlled suspension. To experience it is to understand just how good a car can be; how swiftly but safely you travel, with never a wheel out of place or a trace of drama. Just pleasure."

Lamborghini's tailspin into receivership, along with the new European crash-test regulations, delivered the Silhouette's killing blow, and just over 50 were built. Among the tasks handed to Giulio Alfieri when the receiver appointed him as general manager was to expand Lamborghini's model lineup to attract new owners. In the absence of proper funding to develop a new car, Alfieri opted to rework the Silhouette, the prevailing belief being that the fundamental concept of an affordable open-top Lamborghini was right.

Silhouette P300

Chassis	Steel platform
Suspension	Independent MacPherson front/rear, coil springs, telescopic shock absorbers, anti-roll bars
Brakes	Ventilated Girling discs
Wheelbase	2450 mm
Front/rear track	1484 mm/1532 mm
Wheels/Tires	8 in × 15 in, Pirelli P7 195/15 (front); 11 in × 15 in, Pirelli P7 285/15 (rear)
Engine	Mid-mounted 90-degree V-8
Bore/Stroke	86 mm/64.5 mm
Cubic capacity	2996 cc
Compression ratio	10.1:1
Maximum power	260 bhp at 7500 rpm
Valve gear	Double overhead camshafts, chain drive, 2 valves per cylinder
Fuel/ignition system	4 Weber carburetors, Bendix pump, 2 coils and 1 distributor
Lubrication	Wet sump
Gearbox	Lamborghini 5-speed
Transmission	Rear-wheel drive
Clutch	Dry single-plate, hydraulically assisted
Dry weight	1175 kg
Top speed	161 mph

While Lamborghini was in receivership the Jalpa was developed to woo potential buyers of the company—and potential Lamborghini customers in the US. Revised bodywork included bumpers which complied with US regulations.

While the Silhouette was named after a sportscar racing format, the Jalpa returned to Lamborghini's convention of naming models after fighting bulls. Marc Deschamps at Bertone (who also designed the Athon concept car shown in 1980) revised the styling, neatening the squared-off wheel arches and incorporating US-spec bumpers front and rear—a vital step at a time when the only Lamborghinis making their way to America were doing so by personal import. The interior, though more luxuriously trimmed in leather, was less successful elsewhere. The boxy instrument binnacle met with widespread derision, one magazine suggesting it looked as if the individual dials had been left in their packaging.

To make the engine more suitable for grand touring, Alfieri increased the engine's stroke to 75 millimeters, bringing overall swept capacity to 3,485cc. Peak power remained unchanged at 255 brake horsepower, but the mid-mounted V-8 reached that 500 rpm earlier; more significantly for the car's character, peak torque rose from 130 pound-feet to 232.

How influential the Jalpa was in persuading Mimrans Lamborghini was a growing concern though. That is known only to them, but the car was introduced to the public at the 1981 Geneva motor show, two months after the transfer of assets. Production ran from 1982 to 1988, and while the units produced amounted to 410—modest indeed in comparison to the 12,000-plus Ferrari 308GTBs sold during that car's ten-year life—Lamborghini's last naturally aspirated V-8-powered car played a small but useful role in ensuring the company's future.

Jalpa

Chassis	Steel platform
Suspension	Independent MacPherson front/rear, coil springs, telescopic shock absorbers, anti-roll bars
Brakes	Ventilated Girling discs
Wheelbase	2450 mm
Front/rear track	1500 mm/1554 mm
Wheels/Tires	8 in × 16 in, Pirelli P7 195/16 (front); 11 in × 16 in, Pirelli P7 285/16 (rear)
Engine	Mid-mounted 90-degree V-8
Bore/Stroke	86 mm/75 mm
Cubic capacity	3485 cc
Compression ratio	9.2:1
Maximum power	255 bhp at 7500 rpm
Valve gear	Double overhead camshafts, chain drive, 2 valves per cylinder
Fuel/ignition system	4 Weber carburetors, Bendix pump, 2 coils and 1 distributor
Lubrication	Wet sump
Gearbox	Lamborghini 5-speed
Transmission	Rear-wheel drive
Clutch	Dry single-plate, hydraulically assisted
Dry weight	1435 kg
Top speed	155 mph

DIABLO

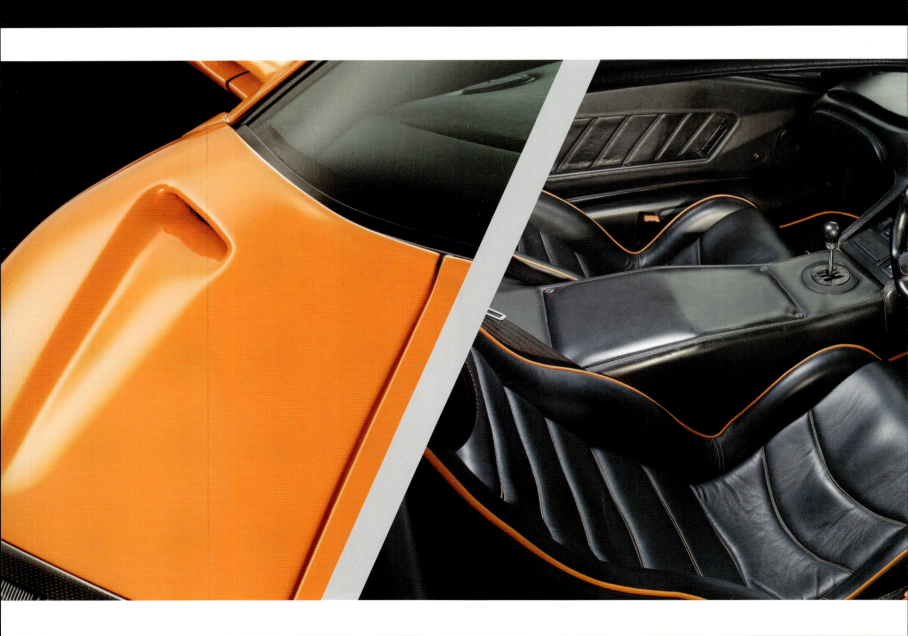

LAMBORGHINI HAD RETURNED TO HEALTH under the Mimran brothers, but it was going to need another round of investment if it was to replace the Jalpa model and, perhaps more importantly, the aging Countach. Though Gandini's remarkable wedge had made a seamless transition across the decades, remaining aloof and aspirational through changing fashions, there were challengers to its crown of unattainability. Ferrari's F40 and Porsche's 959 arrived as genuine 200-miles-per-hour supercars, a Rubicon of speed the draggy Countach was unable to cross.

THE SUPERCAR REFINED

Chrysler's multimillion-dollar acquisition of Lamborghini in April 1987 seemed to guarantee Sant'Agata's future. Nuova Automobili Ferruccio Lamborghini SpA's assets were transferred to a new holding company, Automobili Lamborghini SpA, and a new group of go-ahead directors entered the boardroom, led by Lee Iacocca, the son of Italian immigrants. Iacocca was the poster boy for automotive Reaganomics, having secured massive loans to prop up Chrysler when it was on the brink of bankruptcy in 1978, and subsequently turned the company around. He was used to getting his own way, and when the board meeting decision to purchase Lamborghini was described as "unanimous," you can imagine that the majority of executives present took the career-minded view of agreeing with the boss.

Understandably, the Mimrans had closed down the investment taps in anticipation of the sale, so development of what would become the Diablo stalled when it had barely gotten started. Even so, Chrysler executives set a target of the last quarter of 1988 for the car's launch. This deadline started to slip almost immediately as Chrysler mulled over what it actually wanted Lamborghini to be and how much money it wanted to invest in its new acquisition. The board pondered three options: Lamborghini as a fully self-funded entity; Lamborghini as a halo brand to be added to badge-engineered mass-production "sports" models; or a rapid-growth strategy to bring a still-autonomous Lamborghini up to Ferrari's size quickly, selling more than 2,500 units a year. The first option was dismissed, wisely, on the grounds that it offered insufficient opportunity for growth. Equally wisely, the second option of mounting a branding smash-and-grab was also kicked out, on the grounds that it would quickly devalue the brand—rather like the ghastly Ford Mustangs of the 1980s and '90s.

Diablo VT Roadster

Diablo Roadster

Chassis	Steel spaceframe with composite panels
Suspension	Independent double wishbones front/rear, coil springs and telescopic shock absorbers, anti-roll bars
Brakes	Ventilated Brembo discs
Wheelbase	2650 mm
Front/rear track	1540 mm/1640 mm
Wheels/Tires	17 in × 8.5 in, Pirelli PZero 245/40 (front); 17 in × 13 in, Pirelli PZero 335/35 (rear)
Engine	Rear longitudinal-mounted 60-degree V-12
Bore/Stroke	87 mm/80 mm
Cubic capacity	5707 cc
Compression ratio	10:1
Maximum power	492 bhp at 6800 rpm (claimed)
Valve gear	Dual overhead camshafts, chain drive, 4 valves per cylinder
Fuel/ignition system fuel injection	Dual Bendix pumps, Lamborghini electronic
Lubrication	Wet sump
Gearbox	Lamborghini 5-speed manual
Transmission	Four-wheel drive
Clutch	Dry single-plate
Dry weight	1625 kg
Top speed	201 mph (claimed)

Chief engineer Luigi Marmiroli therefore had a lot of work on his hands. He already had a four-liter V-10 on the bench for the putative new Jalpa, known internally as the P140, and he had to finesse the Countach Anniversary model before restarting the Diablo project. Lamborghini engaged Marcello Gandini to create styling proposals, and by summer 1988 he had produced a full-scale model.

Gandini's proposal did not lack drama, as he relocated the "shoulder" air scoops to the rear deck, with smaller intakes featuring fan-like strakes of diminishing size in the rear three-quarter panel. The side windows plunged downward at the leading edge, and the engine cover was largely glass, while the line of the rear wheelarches swept back toward the taillight cluster, as on Gandini's Citroen BX hatchback.

The arrival of the Cizeta Moroder V-16, a limited-run V-16-engined supercar bankrolled in part by music producer Giorgio Moroder, caused ructions between Gandini and his clients. Gandini had recycled his ideas from the original Diablo proposal into that car while the Diablo was in limbo. Now Chrysler directed him to amend his proposal so that the Diablo would not look too similar when it ultimately hit the streets.

Cizeta would eventually go bust after making just a handful of cars, but in the supercar boom time of the late 1980s nobody could have anticipated that another oil price shock was on the way. The relationship between Sant'Agata and its new paymasters became afflicted with not-invented-here syndrome, and as Gandini and Marmiroli created a working prototype for road testing, the Chrysler executives began to consider getting their own people involved. Lamborghini President Emile Novaro, returning to the business after a serious car accident in 1987, fought to keep his engineers in charge of the project.

The first prototype Diablo, powered by a development of the familiar Quattrovalvole 5.2-liter V-12 and bearing heavy disguise to make it resemble a Countach from a distance, hit the test track at Nardo early in 1989 with Valentino Balboni at the wheel.

Though a clear improvement on the Countach, it still lacked top speed. Marmiroli's team took a two-pronged approach to solving this challenge, aiming for more power and better aerodynamics. Thus, the Bizzarrini V-12 grew again, this time to 5,729 cc, with a bore and stroke of 87 millimeters × 80 millimeters. At the same time, the gearbox was redesigned in a more forward position, offering an even shorter linkage, and the output shaft was relocated to the right so that the driveshaft ran alongside the sump rather than through it.

Chrysler wanted more aesthetic changes and these, somewhat to Gandini's chagrin, were performed by design vice president Tom Gale's team in Detroit. Few could argue with the finished look of the Diablo, though: slightly more soft-edged, less heavy around the hips, and not so slab-sided, with the rear air intakes integrated more neatly and glass replacing the fanned three-quarter panel. It was a design that would survive the passing of time better than the à la mode Cizeta, and Gandini liked it enough to allow his signature to be featured on the flanks of production models.

Gandini's original vision may have been diluted somewhat, but the windtunnel figures spoke for themselves: a drag coefficient of 0.31 compared with the Countach's brick-like 0.42. Unfortunately the Diablo was also heavier, for a number of reasons. It was bigger than the Countach by 6 inches in the wheelbase and was 1.4 inches taller (though still only 43.5 inches high). It was better equipped and more lavishly upholstered, with fully retractable electric-powered windows; their downward slope at the front, retained from Gandini's proposal, gave a much better field of view from the wing mirrors. The mechanical layout of the front end was designed so that the Diablo could be offered in four-wheel-drive form, though the car was rear-wheel drive only until 1992. And crash regulations—particularly in the US—had moved on during the 1980s, so while the chassis followed established Lambo spaceframe practice, it used square tubes rather than round ones, and was reinforced in places with composite panels in an effort to mitigate the weight gain caused by the additional bracing. Likewise, the frame was dressed in aluminum alloy for the doors and quarter panels, and a carbon-glassfiber composite material for the louvered engine cover, hood, and bumpers.

Besides more mod cons for the cabin and a greater quality of fit and finish, contemporary supercar buyers expected a better class of mechanical refinement. That meant abandoning race-style rose joints, and the suspension was redesigned with anti-dive and anti-squat geometry, and to mount to the body via rubber bushes.

The Diablo also gained hidden bulk in the form of the three-way catalytic convertor that was now mandatory in most markets. In turn, that meant the 5.7-liter V-12 bid farewell to the Weber family of carburetors that had served so well, replaced by a new Weber-Magnetti Marelli multipoint fuel injection system.

The question on most testers' lips, then, as the Diablo charged out of the gates at a gala Monte Carlo launch in January 1990, was whether the greater muscle (from 455 brake horsepower in the outgoing Countach to 492 brake horsepower) and slipperier aero could outweigh the 361 pounds it had gained over its predecessor. This was a critical moment; two weeks before the Diablo's launch, Ferrari announced it had gained type approval to export some of the F40 production run to the United States.

Deliveries began in September, and the initial response was largely positive. Peter Robinson, *Autocar* magazine's European editor, wrote:

> Lamborghini's new Diablo is a supercar of stirring contrasts: an outrageous and extravagant car so intense in its emotions and personality no Japanese manufacturer would ever contemplate production of such a vehicle. Contradictions abound, flaws are both plentiful and obvious—and a couple are unforgiveable—but as a successor to the legendary Countach, Lamborghini has the Diablo's priorities appropriately apportioned.
>
> A Ferrari Testarossa's 390bhp is but a wimp in comparison with an engine that pumps out 492bhp at 7000rpm, and an even more impressive 428lb ft of torque at 5200rpm. . . . The fluency of its turbine-like sound at low revs highlights a smoothness that is only matched by the very best large-capacity, multi-cylinder motorcycle engines.

Diablo SV

Diablo

Chassis	Steel spaceframe with composite panels
Suspension	Independent double wishbones front/rear, coil springs and telescopic shock absorbers, anti-roll bars
Brakes	Ventilated Brembo discs
Wheelbase	2650 mm
Front/rear track	1540 mm/1640 mm
Wheels/Tires	17 in × 8.5 in, Pirelli PZero 245/40 (front); 17 in × 13 in, Pirelli PZero 335/35 (rear)
Engine	Rear longitudinal-mounted 60-degree V-12
Bore/Stroke	87 mm/80 mm
Cubic capacity	5707 cc
Compression ratio	10:1
Maximum power	492 bhp at 6800 rpm (claimed)
Valve gear	Dual overhead camshafts, chain drive, 4 valves per cylinder
Fuel/ignition system	Dual Bendix pumps, Lamborghini electronic fuel injection
Lubrication	Wet sump
Gearbox	Lamborghini 5-speed manual
Transmission	Two-wheel drive
Clutch	Dry single-plate
Dry weight	1576 kg
Top speed	204 mph (claimed)

Diablo SE

Chassis	Steel spaceframe with composite panels
Suspension	Independent double wishbones front/rear, coil springs and telescopic shock absorbers, anti-roll bars
Brakes	Ventilated Brembo discs
Wheelbase	2650 mm
Front/rear track	1540 mm/1640 mm
Wheels/Tires	17 in × 8.5 in, Pirelli PZero 245/40 (front); 17 in × 13 in, Pirelli PZero 335/35 (rear)
Engine	Rear longitudinal-mounted 60-degree V-12
Bore/Stroke	87 mm/80 mm
Cubic capacity	5707 cc
Compression ratio	10:1
Maximum power	492 bhp at 6800 rpm (claimed)
Valve gear	Dual overhead camshafts, chain drive, 4 valves per cylinder
Fuel/ignition system	Dual Bendix pumps, Lamborghini electronic fuel injection
Lubrication	Wet sump
Gearbox	Lamborghini 5-speed manual
Transmission	Two-wheel drive
Clutch	Dry single-plate
Dry weight	1451 kg
Top speed	205 mph (claimed)

The Chrysler-designed interior met with approval, though the style would date rather quickly, but as with Lamborghinis past the footwells were too narrow and the ergonomics suboptimal.

"The trouble is the wheel juts out on a long column," wrote Robinson, "and its thick rim does its very best to hide the top row of small dials and splits the speedo and tacho in half. The entire binnacle is adjustable, as is the wheel, but the range available only allows you to decide which dials you prefer to be hidden."

No road testers were able to find a clear enough stretch of asphalt to test Lamborghini's claimed 202 miles per hour (which the indefatigable Balboni has since admitted he achieved with the mirrors and windscreen wipers removed and no rear wing, which must have been an interesting experience at Nardi's curved circuit). But

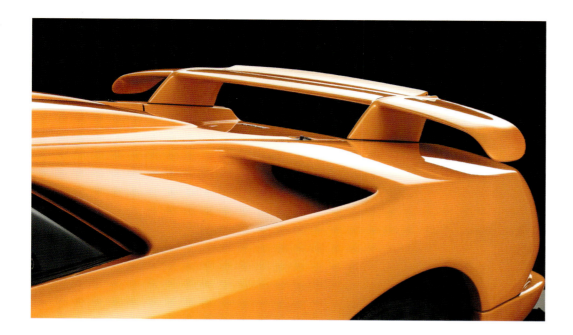

there were no complaints about the car's performance characteristics or general attitude. The main flaw, as Robinson pointed out, was the steering, which lacked self-centering action and was often too heavy.

Regardless of how the Diablo rated in comparison with its rivals, events on the geopolitical stage in 1990 would have a greater effect on it and the health of the company. Japan's stock market crashed after the government took belated action to rein in an economy that was in the grip of a speculative bubble. Many major European markets also lurched into recession. On August 2, tensions in the Middle East came to a head as Iraq invaded neighboring Kuwait, causing the price of crude oil per barrel to more than double. After the excess of the 1980s, the hangover had set in. Conspicuous consumption in the form of supercar ownership fell out of fashion, walloping sales of the Diablo and many others of its ilk.

Chrysler was also in trouble. In the boom years it had tried to diversify by acquiring the likes of Gulfstream Aerospace as well as Lamborghini and the American Motors Corporation, but these had saddled the company with huge debts; it sold Gulfstream in 1989, but this wasn't enough to alleviate its financial difficulties.

Although the Diablo had a healthy post-launch order book, by the time deliveries began in September 1990 Chrysler had already tasked the investment bank J.P. Morgan with sounding out potential buyers for Lamborghini. Word soon got around the auto industry that the company was up for sale once more, with obvious consequences for morale at Sant'Agata.

Worse still, early Diablos suffered overheating problems and fading brakes, along with generally indifferent build quality. With onward investment from Chrysler drying up—the Formula 1 engine project was left to wither on the vine, and the new building to house the P140 production line would remain empty for years—Lamborghini management redeployed staff from P140 development to get the Diablo build sorted. The "baby Lambo" project would remain in stasis for the better part of a decade.

Gandini produced an open-top Roadster prototype with a cut-down windshield for the 1992 Geneva Motor Show, but this model would not be built on Chrysler's watch. Instead, Lamborghini used its scant resources to finalize the all-wheel-drive Diablo VT for launch the following year. The center-mounted viscous coupling (derived from the unloved LM002 off-roader) directed up to 25 percent of the engine's torque to the front wheels when the rears broke traction—an occurrence that required the driver to operate on a spectrum in the gray area between bravery and stupidity. The four-wheel-drive hardware added weight, but since the intrusive transmission tunnel was common to all Diablos, it had no further effect on a footwell so tight that drivers with feet bigger than a size 10 often had to remove a shoe. Mechanical improvements common to both Diablo models included a new nose treatment that improved front-brake ventilation, uprated calipers, electronically adjustable dampers, power steering, and a dashboard where most of the instruments were visible.

Unsold Diablos piled up during the recession and the company hemorrhaged money while unionized staff members were paid to arrive and do little work. Over in Detroit, changing politics in the boardroom eroded Iacocca's power, and he was edged into retirement at the end of 1992. Any will to retain Lamborghini followed him out the door.

In January 1994 a consortium of three Bermuda-based, Indonesian-owned companies, all of which had ownership ties to Hutomo "Tommy" Mandala Putra—the son of Indonesian President Suharto—and multimillionaire Setiawan Djody paid a reported $40 million for Lamborghini. A lead article in the New York Times asked, "Is the purchase of Italy's Lamborghini a $40 million toy for the son of Indonesia's President Suharto and his friends or rather the core of a Malaysian-Indonesian joint venture to create a local automotive industry?" The author took a straw poll among analysts and concluded that the former was most likely. "'It's plausible, but you have to ask whether this is the most cost-efficient way to start an industry,' said Louis Bailoni, luxury-car analyst with DRI Automotive Group in Britain. 'It would make a lot more sense to just go out and buy the engines you want for your cars.' Another London auto analyst, asking not to be named, said that buying Lamborghini in order to launch a local car industry was 'ludicrous' and 'a very strange way of doing it.'"

Djody had big plans to create a new car for the Indonesian market under the Megatech brand, along with a new Lamborghini semi-amphibious vehicle to be called the Borneo. He and Suharto installed former Lotus, Jaguar, and General Motors executive Mike Kimberley to run Sant'Agata, and a most peculiar epoch began.

As the global economic outlook started to improve, Lamborghini celebrated its 30th anniversary in 1994 with a race-style limited-edition Diablo, the SE30. In the grand supercar tradition of offering less while charging more, the SE30 went without luxuries such as the air con, stereo, power steering, and electric windows, while the side glass was also exchanged for fixed plexiglass with an inset sliding vent. Composite bucket seats and multipoint harnesses added to the stripped-out racer feel, while a revised (and noisier) exhaust, new inlet manifolds, and different fuel metering helped liberate more horses, taking engine power to 523 brake horsepower. One hundred and fifty SE30s are believed to have been built, of which around 15 were converted to an out-and-out race spec by means of a factory "Jota" conversion kit that included, among other hardcore modifications, an even louder exhaust for those owners determined to cultivate tinnitus.

We say "believed" and "around" because during the Megatech era, for reasons unknown, many of Lamborghini's historical documents were consigned to the shredder. Sales and production figures have had to be pieced together subsequently from other sources.

As with previous heads of the company, Kimberley identified that Lamborghini needed to offer more than one core model to turn a profit. The bottom line was that it had to build more cars, and Kimberley announced plans to double production. He was starting from a low base—little more than 200 Diablos were departing Sant'Agata per year.

To broaden the Diablo's appeal, Lamborghini introduced a new entry-level model at the 1995 Geneva show. The SV badge harkened back to the Miura era and combined a modest power hike (to 510 brake horsepower) with two-wheel drive and an adjustable rear spoiler. The much-delayed Diablo VT Roadster arrived at the Bologna Motor Show at the end of 1995, and featured bespoke 17-inch magnesium wheels and a targa roof that mounted above the engine lid when removed.

By early 1996 Kimberley was briefing journalists that the owners planned to invest $155 million in the coming years to fund the new off-roader, a "baby Diablo," and a "new Diablo" that would probably be a reworked version of the existing car. This investment never arrived and the new products remained largely on paper, though Zagato, Gandini, and Italdesign produced prototypes for the proposed volume model.

Kimberley had also recruited a clutch of British designers and engineers he had worked with in the past, including McLaren F1 stylist Peter Stevens, and their arrival was greeted with as much suspicion as the Chrysler-led American invasion of the late 1980s. Very little of his planned new model push would come to fruition, though, because even though sales improved the company was still operating in the red. The owners restructured the ownership of Lamborghini among their various companies, and in August 1996 recruited Fiat executive Vittorio Di Capua as joint vice president with a mandate to cut costs. He and Kimberley failed to agree on financial projections, and Kimberley, who felt that the owners had lost confidence in him, handed in his notice that November. Di Capua was promoted to CEO.

Di Capua pushed on with cost-cutting measures, and the axe swung on several senior managers. Others, including Marmiroli, sought employment with better long-term prospects elsewhere, though very able engineers such as Massimo Ceccarani remained on the engineering team. But when the Indonesian economy crashed as part of the wider Asian financial crisis in 1997 (during which President Suharto was driven from office), Lamborghini found itself trapped in its own corporate Groundhog Day, repeating the hand-to-mouth financial traumas of the late 1970s.

Diablo VT

Salvation arrived in the form of the Volkswagen Group, which had not only weathered the various economic slowdowns of recent years but had added some of the casualties—such as Bugatti—to its war chest. In trying to restart the P140 project within a reasonable timeframe and budget, Di Capua had entered tentative negotiations with Audi, one of VAG's premium brands, to use its V-8 engine and well-regarded Quattro all-wheel drivetrain in the P140.

At that time VAG was the fiefdom of Ferdinand Piëch, grandson of Ferdinand Porsche and chief engineer of the iconic Porsche 917 sports car. Piëch cultivated an interest in acquiring Audi—he was on something of a shopping spree, since VAG was in the process of buying Bentley—and after protracted negotiations Lamborghini came in to Audi ownership in the summer of 1998 for a sum estimated to be in the region of $18 million.

If anyone had misgivings about the direction the company would take under its new owners—and whether Audi was committed to the level of investment required to make Lamborghini strong again—those misgivings would be dispelled over the coming years,

as detailed in later chapters of this book. Audi quickly set out a new model program but also, in the grand tradition of Lamborghini run-out models, reengineered many elements of the Diablo to create the most extreme variant yet.

The SV, VT, and Roadster models were facelifted, with a new cabin and a front-end treatment featuring lights sourced from Nissan's parts bin to replace the old pop-up units, and revised suspension geometry and tuning to improve its on-road demeanor. Eighteen-inch wheels allowed bigger brake rotors to be fitted, and ABS joined the equipment list. Power output rose to 529 brake horsepower.

At the Frankfurt Motor Show, Audi unveiled the limited-edition GT model, a wild race-bred variant with extensive carbon fiber, three-piece OZ wheels, and a roof-mounted engine air intake. Stretched to six liters, the V-12 generated 575 brake horsepower at 7300 rpm—at which point, thanks to a revised exhaust system, everyone within a radius of several miles would know about it. Collectors snapped up the 80 examples of this very quickly, and demand was also high for the race-ready GTR variant that Audi showed at Bologna. Even more rare—only 40 units would be built—the GTR had a full roll cage, Speedline wheels, and a race exhaust, and its engine was tuned to 590 brake horsepower via the addition of a sophisticated new inlet system with variable valve timing. Some of this car's more carefree owners even raced it in the Lamborghini Super Trofeo, a one-make series organized by the promoters of the FIA GT Championship.

For the 2000 model year Audi placed the six-liter engine in the standard VT in a milder state of tune (543 brake horsepower), made some further cosmetic changes, and managed to free up more space in the footwells. Changing the pedal box required some retooling but served as a signal of intent that from now on the driver accommodation would no longer be an afterthought.

There was no doubt that the final Diablo was the best yet, but in some aspects it was still behind the times—and its leading competitors—as related by Larry Webster in a July 2000 *Road & Track* magazine test of the VT:

> Despite the fact the rear tires—Z-rated Pirelli P Zeros, good for more than 200 mph—are so wide that, at first glance, they appear to form a solid rolling pin of rubber across the rear of the car, 543 horses and 457 pound-feet of torque can reduce them to pudding. To counter that possibility, the Diablo VT's four-wheel-drive system makes perfect sense. A viscous coupling transfers power to the front wheels if the rears slip; the rest of the time, the Diablo prowls about as a rear-drive car. At most, 28 percent of engine torque is routed to the front wheels. There are no levers to switch or buttons to punch to engage this four-wheel-drive system, and during routine driving, you'd never know this wild Italian was a four-wheeler.

Perform a drag-strip launch, however, and you'll instantly realize the Diablo VT is not a rear-driver. Usually, those of us who drive in hard acceleration tests rely on a touch of wheelspin to get the car moving in the quickest manner. In a four-wheel-drive car with sticky tires, it is almost impossible to get those rears spinning in a hard launch, unless the car has a system that allows some initial rear wheelspin before the fronts get the juice. An example of one such car is the 1997 Porsche 911 Turbo S. Hold the gas pedal down to create 4500rpm in that sports car, then drop the clutch, and the rear tires will spin for a moment before power is directed to the front wheels; the tires dig in and you're off. In that Porsche, we've recorded 0-to-60-mph blasts in an amazingly fast 3.7 seconds.

But we've tested just one Diablo VT before (C/D, September 1994), because they are very tough to come by—just 23 were sold in the U.S. in 1999, apparently to people who own small countries or athletic shoe companies, at a price of about $275,000. At that test, we declined to risk the dropped-clutch technique, figuring the Diablo's massive tires (235/40ZR-17s up front and 335/35ZR-17s at the rear) and substantial weight (3900 pounds) would result in gobs of traction and no wheelspin. More to the point, there's a good chance that revving the engine and dumping the clutch would fry the clutch and possibly destroy it, and we did not want to find out what that repair bill would look like. A good guess is somewhere in the vicinity of $9000.

The inability to spin the wheels of your Diablo to achieve an optimal getaway compared with a Porsche sounds like the epitome of a first-world problem. But traction-compromised enthusiasts need not have worried: better launches were just part of the package of improvements that would flow from the revitalized Sant'Agata in coming years.

Diablo 6.0

Chassis	Steel spaceframe with composite panels
Suspension	Independent double wishbones front/rear, coil springs and telescopic shock absorbers, anti-roll bars
Brakes	Ventilated Brembo discs
Wheelbase	2650 mm
Front/rear track	1610 mm/1670 mm
Wheels/Tires	18 in × 8.5 in, Pirelli PZero 245/35 (front); 18 in × 13 in, Pirelli PZero 335/40 (rear)
Engine	Rear longitudinal-mounted 60-degree V-12
Bore/Stroke	87 mm/84 mm
Cubic capacity	5992 cc
Compression ratio	10.7:1
Maximum power	492 bhp at 6800 rpm (claimed)
Valve gear	Dual overhead camshafts, chain drive, 4 valves per cylinder
Fuel/ignition system	Lamborghini electronic fuel injection
Lubrication	Wet sump
Gearbox	Lamborghini 5-speed manual
Transmission	Four-wheel drive
Clutch	Dry single-plate
Dry weight	1625 kg
Top speed	205 mph (claimed)

LAMBORGHINI IN FORMULA 1

Anyone who had sneaked in under the Estoril fence that day in September 1993 would have known something strange was going on. Plain white car, driver in a distinctive yellow and green helmet, bellowing multi-cylinder engine: Ayrton Senna was testing the McLaren Lamborghini.

Sadly, this wasn't to be the beginning of a great journey, but the beginning of the end.

The timing of Chrysler's acquisition of Lamborghini had coincided with a period of unease about the dominance of turbocharged engines in Formula 1 motor racing. Motorsport's governing body, the FIA, was progressively clamping down, imposing fuel capacity and boost pressure limits, then announcing an outright ban from the 1989 season onward.

Late in 1987 Gerard Larrousse, twice a winner at the Le Mans 24 Hours and founder of his eponymous F1 team, approached former Ferrari designer Mauro Forghieri with a view to him designing an F1 engine with Lamborghini backing. Sant'Agata, flush with the prospect of new investment, bought in to the idea and established a new division, Lamborghini Engineering, to build the engine.

The new F1 V-12—an 80-degree design, unrelated to the venerable Bizzarrini one—was ready by mid-1988 and duly made its race debut in the back of Larrousse's pair of Lola chassis at the Autódromo Internacional Nelson Piquet in March 1989. Lamborghini's involvement was purposefully low-key, working with a mid-ranking team purely as a supplier, and doing so at arm's length thanks to the existence of Lamborghini Engineering.

Even so, the season was a disappointment. Philippe Alliot scored the team's only points finish in Spain, while a revolving door policy held sway in the adjoining garage: Yannick Dalmas, a promising talent before falling victim to Legionnaire's disease in 1988, failed to qualify on several occasions before being "let go"; Eric Bernard stood in for two races before retreating back to F3000; and then former title challenger Michele Alboreto completed the final eight rounds without troubling the points.

Lamborghini's own official history places the blame at Larrousse's door: "The fault for these poor results lay above all with the French team, which did not have the money and organization required to compete at the highest levels." Fair enough, but the engine was overweight and not best reliable, as demonstrated on more than one occasion, not least when Bernard's blew up as he was running fifth at Silverstone.

Still, the engine had potential, and since the only other ones available to customers at an affordable rate were demonstrably puny V-8s, Lamborghini gained Lotus as a customer for 1990. With development came results, the best of which was Aguri Suzuki's podium finish in front of his home crowd at Suzuka in the maligned Larrousse.

Lamborghini was also proceeding at full steam with its own F1 chassis, commissioned by an ambitious young Mexican businessman named Fernando Gonzalez Luna. The GLAS (Gonzalez Luna Associates) consortium raised a claimed $20 million from sponsors before the man himself vanished without trace, along with the money, in the summer of 1990. Faced with a choice between throwing good money after bad or junking the entire project, Lamborghini chose the former, but strictly limited the amount of cash it injected into the car and the team that would run it, somehow persuading Italian financier and industrialist Carlo Petrucco to get involved.

Thus, an entity named Modena Team arrived at the opening Grand Prix of the 1991 season with a pair of metallic blue cars badged as Lamborghini 291s. In spite of having to complete pre-qualifying—there were so many entries in those days that the minnows were pruned viciously in a knock-out session on the Friday morning of each grand prix weekend—the cars showed potential. Nicola Larini finished seventh at Phoenix, and Eric van de Poele was in the points and had the checkered flag almost in sight at Imola when his fuel pump broke.

But in Formula 1, if you don't invest in going forward you end up going backward, hence the truism that the fastest way to make a small fortune in motor racing is to start off with a large one. With no more money forthcoming—Lamborghini's official history blames Chrysler, but that's being a trifle economical with the *actualité*—Modena Team barely registered its presence again and shuttered its doors at the end of the season.

From 1992 the Lamborghini name was joined by Chrysler branding on customer engine covers, although the continuing underperformance of those customers led the US giant to wonder if it was all worthwhile. An opportunity to test that theory would soon arrive.

In 1993 McLaren was in trouble, soldiering on after Honda's withdrawal from F1 with customer Ford engines. This did not sit well with Senna, the team's star driver, who nonetheless pulled out a string of epic against-the-odds race wins while still refusing to consider anything more than a race-by-race contract. Senna wanted more power. Team boss Ron Dennis was desperate to retain his champion. Opportunity, in the form of Chrysler, knocked.

That summer a small team at McLaren's base in Woking, England, worked solidly for three months to adapt a chassis designed to accommodate a Ford V-8 so that it would accept Lamborghini's raging V-12 leviathan. This was no cut-and-shut job; the transmission, drive-by-wire throttle, and all the other control electronics were painstakingly adapted so that when the car ran, it would be representative.

And when it did, in a secret test at Estoril in Portugal, Senna was so enthused that he immediately phoned Dennis: more power in the midrange, a little less manic at the top, and McLaren could race it straight away. Forghieri duly removed 25 brake horsepower from the top of the rev range but created a peak of 60 brake horsepower more than before in the rump.

Dennis shook hands on a deal with Chrysler's Bob Lutz and Lamborghini Engineering's Daniele Audetto at the Frankfurt Motor Show that September. Weeks later, Senna tested the Lambo-engined McLaren again at Silverstone, pronounced himself satisfied with the changes, again entreated Dennis to race it before the end of the season, then handed over driving duties to Mika Hakkinen. Fittingly for what was about to happen next, after a handful of laps the engine suffered a devastating blow-up.

The McLaren-Chrysler partnership never reached the contract stage. Dennis chose Peugeot instead, Senna left McLaren for the dominant Williams team, Chrysler sold Lamborghini, and the adventure was over.

Diablo VT

Chassis	Steel spaceframe with composite panels
Suspension	Independent double wishbones front/rear, coil springs and telescopic shock absorbers, anti-roll bars
Brakes	Ventilated Brembo discs
Wheelbase	2650 mm
Front/rear track	1540 mm/1640 mm
Wheels/Tires	17 in × 8.5 in, Pirelli PZero 245/40 (front); 17 in × 13 in, Pirelli PZero 335/35 (rear)
Engine	Rear longitudinal-mounted 60-degree V-12
Bore/Stroke	87 mm/80 mm
Cubic capacity	5707 cc
Compression ratio	10:1
Maximum power	492 bhp at 6800 rpm (claimed)
Valve gear	Dual overhead camshafts, chain drive, 4 valves per cylinder
Fuel/ignition system	Dual Bendix pumps, Lamborghini electronic fuel injection
Lubrication	Wet sump
Gearbox	Lamborghini 5-speed manual
Transmission	Four-wheel drive
Clutch	Dry single-plate
Dry weight	1625 kg
Top speed	202 mph (claimed)

MURCIÉLAGO

DURING THE COURSE OF SATURDAY, SEPTEMBER 8, 2001, some 200 Lamborghinis came home to the factory at Sant'Agata Bolognese, steered with almost breathless excitement down the Autostrada by their eager owners, each one anxious to see what the first Lamborghini developed under Audi's ownership would look like. There had been spy photos, of course. But this would be it: the Murciélago in the metal.

AUDI FLEXES ITS MUSCLE

A remarkable 4,099 Murciélagos were built during its nine-year production run—double the number the Countach achieved between 1974 and 1990.

The last of the daylight had faded when the guests—owners, wealthy enthusiasts, VIPs—were directed to a corner of the factory where a temporary stage had been erected. The lights came down. The opening bars of Steppenwolf's *Born to Be Wild* pounded through the speakers, soon joined by the familiar roar of the Lambo V-12 as an example of the new car was revealed—resplendent in eye-popping Verde Ithica paintwork. Grown men would later claim to have shed real tears upon seeing it for the first time. Beatlemania had nothing on this.

The night before, the Murciélago had been unveiled to selected media in what lives in the memory of those scribes privileged to be present as one of the most flamboyant press junkets of all time: at night, on the slopes of Mount Etna, with pyrotechnics, fake lava flows, specially commissioned films, and live dancers.

"The volcano was smoking gently as we flew in," the editor of *Car* magazine, Angus Mackenzie, would later write. "And as we drove up the mountain some of the lava from an eruption mere weeks earlier was still cooling. It wasn't hard to figure out the subtext here: This car is meant to be intimidating. Handle with care."

Since the due diligence process had made it clear that Lamborghini needed to sell 1,500 cars a year to remain a viable business, Audi had set an ambitious timeframe for new models. Replacing the Diablo would be the priority, with a greater-volume "baby Lambo" to follow within a minimum of two years after the Diablo's successor. Moving in to the factory in August 1998 to revealing the finished Murciélago to potential buyers took just over three years.

The easy option would have been to push on with whatever was already in development. But before, during, and after the transition from Chrysler to Megatech ownership, Lamborghini vacillated on product development, and the result was a clutch of proposals that were not pursued. In the early 1990s, Marcello Gandini was invited to design a replacement for the Jalpa, but his angular and rather '80s proposal was not much liked. Italdesign's Calà also came and went; McLaren F1 stylist Peter Stevens, doing contract work in Sant'Agata, described it as so: "Not one of their best pieces of work, it was a fat and not a particularly cohesive design." Then Zagato showed a supposedly production-ready concept based on the Diablo chassis and drivetrain (albeit without the ABS and traction control) and called the Raptor at Geneva in 1996, but it was not taken up, either. Instead, Zagato had been invited to produce a new design, and development of the putative new car—known as the Canto—was well underway when Lamborghini changed hands again in 1998. Spy photographs of a development "mule" undergoing testing at Nardo had already been published in several European car magazines.

VW Group boss Ferdinand Piëch scrutinized the Canto and, like a Roman emperor adjudicating an unsatisfactory gladiatorial bout, gave it the thumbs-down. Only the chassis, engine, and drivetrain would be retained. Work progressed quickly; Audi invited styling proposals from other leading Italian design houses, including Bertone and Giugiaro's Italdesign, and seconded its own Luc Donkerwolke to establish an in-house design office at Sant'Agata.

By the time the second-generation Murciélago came on stream in 2006, build quality was well up to Audi standards.

Donkerwolke was seen as an unusual choice by many, since the majority of his work had been in the more humdrum field—he had only recently returned to Audi after a tenure at Skoda, the VW Group's Czech-based value brand, where he had helped style the company's first new ground-up designs under VW's ownership. But the gifted and ambitious Belgian was determined to make his mark on cars with a sticker price bearing considerably more decimal places. By the beginning of 2000, after considering all the proposals, Audi had signed off on the design by Donkerwolke's team.

The triumph of the Murciélago is that it established a fresh set of design cues for the 21st century while carrying enough familiar features to avoid frightening Lamborghini purists. Since its chassis was a development of the Diablo's, it's no surprise to see they shared a similar stance and proportions, though the newer car rebalanced the cabin and glasshouse away from the "cab forward" look that had been so modish in the late 1980s and early 1990s. The gaping shoulder vents that had offended the eyes of Piëch and his senior engineers as they contemplated the later Diablos and the Canto were gone, replaced by subtly aero-optimized scoops. This new car embraced Lamborghini's past rather than seeking to put them through the shredder along with the company files; why, even the front shutline of its scissor doors clearly echoed those of the Diablo.

It was fresh yet familiar, neat and modern but far from dull—a car that could, like all Lambo supercars past, command attention, as documented by John Phillips in *Car and Driver*:

> On I-94 in front of Detroit Metro Airport, I tried to pass a Melvindale Elementary school bus. As I drew even, I noticed the bus had started

to lean at a frightening angle—was leaning in my direction, in fact, like a yellow Lusitania about to invert. I nailed the throttle to avoid being crushed. As I roared past, I could see the driver was half out of his seat, his body twisted to the left, his face contorted. He looked like Ralph Kramden yelling at Ed Norton. Here was his problem: Every child onboard had stampeded to the portside windows.

That little dancing bull on the nose of a car—it drives people nuts.

The faithfulness to Lamborghini's past was reflected in the car's choice of name. Audi dropped the "Canto" tag and scoured the history books for a suitably named Miura bull, eventually alighting upon Murciélago, a particularly resilient bovine that came into Don Antonio Miura's hands when its life was spared after it withstood many stabbings in the ring during a fight in 1879 (as with so much associated with Lamborghini folklore, the exact number of stabbings is hotly debated). There was something appropriate, given Lamborghini's recent financial health, about naming the company's new big beast thus.

Murciélago

Chassis	Tubular steel monocoque with composite inserts
Suspension	Independent double wishbones front/rear, coaxial coil springs, telescopic self-adjusting shock absorbers, anti-roll bars, and anti-squat bars
Brakes	Ventilated Brembo discs with ABS and DRP
Wheelbase	2665 mm
Front/rear track	1635 mm/1695 mm
Wheels/Tires	18 in × 8.5 in, Pirelli PZero 245/35 (front); 18 in × 13 in, Pirelli PZero 335/30 (rear)
Engine	Rear longitudinal-mounted 60-degree V-12
Bore/Stroke	87 mm/86.6 mm
Cubic capacity	6192 cc
Compression ratio	10.7:1
Maximum power	580 bhp at 7500 rpm
Valve gear	Dual overhead camshafts, chain drive, 4 valves per cylinder, continuously variable timing
Fuel/ignition system	Lamborghini electronic fuel injection, individual coils
Lubrication	Dry sump
Gearbox	Lamborghini 6-speed manual (e-gear robotized manual optional)
Transmission	Four-wheel drive
Clutch	Dry single-plate
Dry weight	1650 kg (Roadster 1665 kg)
Top speed	205 mph (Roadster 199 mph)

Manufacture of the steel tube frame was outsourced at first, with the composite body panels produced in-house along with the roof panel, which as a load-bearing element was made of steel. Engineering director Massimo Ceccarani oversaw an interesting departure in the engine bay, stretching the venerable V-12 to 6.2 liters and dry-sumping it, as Giotto Bizzarrini had originally intended. This enabled the unit to be installed 50 millimeters lower, with obvious handling benefits.

Lamborghini retained its own four-wheel-drive transmission rather than adopting Audi's famous Quattro system, and the new six-speed gearbox—a first for Lamborghini—was also developed in-house at Sant'Agata. As before, the rear differential was integral to the block, with a viscous coupling directing drive to the front wheels. Lamborghini also introduced a paddle-shift gearbox called the e-gear, which was not a semi-automatic but a robotized manual. This system continues to divide opinion among owners.

The brakes featured ABS for the first time, but even though this was the most thoroughly tested new Lambo ever, braking was repeatedly highlighted as a weak spot by professional testers and owners. Many of the latter had third-party upgrades fitted, especially those who drove the car as Balboni intended.

Simon George, a track day organizer who acquired a Murciélago for his company to run, detailed the expenses involved in running the car for several years in *Evo* magazine. In one entry he nails the brake issue:

> A couple of weeks ago I got a welcome call from Renato Cappucci, managing director of Tarox UK. Regular readers may recall that I needed some new brake discs, as the old ones were starting to crack. At a grand [English slang for £1000] a corner, I passed on Lamborghini's own discs, made by Brembo and unobtainable elsewhere. Instead I let Tarox have a couple of my worn ones, which were then sent to the company's factory in Italy to act as templates for a new set. Three weeks later and Tarox came up trumps with beautifully machined replacements that had been grooved instead of drilled to avoid the cracking issue.
>
> First impressions are very positive, with significantly more bite on offer. There's a bit of squealing while they're bedding in, but it's a small price to pay for reduced fade on track. At £1500 a set they make the £4000 being asked for the OE [original equipment] items look very expensive.

To balance performance with looks, the Murciélago featured a number of movable components that only deployed when needed, including a rear spoiler that self-erected to 50 degrees above 80 miles per hour, then to 70 degrees at 135 miles per hour. The air intakes on each shoulder also rose when the engine required more cooling—or, via a switch in the cockpit, when the driver wanted to show off.

LUC DONCKERWOLKE

The son of a Belgian diplomat, Luc Donckerwolke was born in Lima, Peru, in 1965, and spent his early years globetrotting around Africa and South America. The experience made him fluently multilingual.

He completed his education in Europe, studying industrial engineering and transportation design at institutions in Belgium and Switzerland, and got his break in the automotive industry at Peugeot in 1990. In 1992 he moved to Audi and thus began a lightning procession up the design ladder in the Volkswagen Group, which he has attributed to being an "outsider."

"I became the designer for special projects," he told one interviewer. "Most of my colleagues were linear designers who wanted to stay with single projects so they could go home at four. I never went home."

After two years at Audi he moved to Skoda, the Czech brand acquired by VW in the late 1980s and then undergoing a relaunch. By 1996 he was back at Audi, contributing to the radical all-aluminum A2 and the styling buck of what would become the R8R Le Mans race car.

His secondment to Lamborghini, acquired by Audi in 1998, afforded him a great opportunity. He facelifted the Diablo for its final SV incarnation and sold senior management on his vision for its successor, beating off proposals from the likes of Bertone, Italdesign, and IDEA. During this time Lamborghini established its own styling department, Centro Stile.

Donckerwolke worked with Italdesign on the Gallardo, and supervised the Murciélago Roadster, before being redeployed to the VW Group's Spanish brand SEAT as head of design. In 2012 he was promoted again to head up design at Bentley, another of VW's flagship acquisitions.

While Audi had removed some of the ergonomic quirks typically associated with Lamborghini—although the manifest difficulty of reversing such a substantial vehicle in tight spaces, with limited visibility, would remain—the carryover nature of the chassis from the Diablo made for some unavoidable inconveniences. As John Phillips noted in *Car and Driver*: "What you notice first about the Murciélago is that its left-front wheel intrudes some eight inches into prime footwell territory, skewing your feet to the right. Your left foot searches for a place to relax—under the clutch is about the only comfortable spot. What you notice next is the accelerator pedal juts out of a small black box, like a paddle raised in a canoe. Your heel rests on the front of this box, and you bend your toes forward to move the throttle. You can duplicate the sensation by walking around with a box of Tic Tacs in your shoe."

Prospective owners were not dissuaded. In 2000 Lamborghini sold 296 Diablos. Once the Murciélago came on stream, the figure rose to 424 units in 2002. But the company was still a long way from break-even territory—to reach that it would need the more affordable Gallardo. Still, it continued to refresh the Murciélago throughout its life, ensuring that annual sales of that model would only dip below the 400 mark once until 2009.

A roadster variant was the obvious way to broaden the Murciélago's appeal, and once the Gallardo was signed off, Donckerwolke got to work. Lamborghini showed a concept at the Detroit show in 2003, then unveiled the Murciélago Roadster for real at Geneva in March 2004, alongside a limited-edition version of the coupe model (distinguished by a one-off exterior color in blue, different wheels, leather trim, new exhaust, and a numbered plaque inside), of which 50 were built, to celebrate the company's 40th anniversary.

The eye-catching interior featured different material for the driver's side, in a perforated finish, to make it "extreme and exclusive," said Donckerwolke. You could even specify each side of the cabin in a different shade of leather, if you wished.

To regain the structural stiffness lost with the roof, the Roadster gained additional box-section steel tubes in strategic places, with additional composite elements in the A-pillars and the sills. For rollover protection, the windshield frame was beefed up, and a pair of pop-up roll bars from the Audi parts bin were installed behind the headrests. A steel engine brace ran over the V-12 from rear bulkhead to the suspension carriers, though for an extra $4,000 this could be had in carbon fiber. In a neat and purposeful nod to history, the engine cover itself hinged from the rear, as its equivalent did on the Miura.

The Roadster was supplied with a very basic canvas lid that was not so much a roof as a *bonnet de douche*—and one not warranted to be used at speeds over 100 miles per hour at that. Douglas Kott described the driving experience in *Road & Track*:

> Top removed, the throbbing, slightly reedy backfill of the V-12's exhaust tingles your very core for the complete THX-Dolby theater experience . . . in a theater whose viscous-coupling all-wheel drive channels the engine's 572bhp for a 0-60 blast of about 3.8 seconds. With the wind tugging at your hair and tearing at your face, it seems quicker still.
>
> You *could* use the top, but it's really designed to protect the leather-clad interior from the freak cloudburst. It's a fussy contraption, with a collapsible small-gauge steel tube frame, that needs to be unfolded, extended, fitted, and snapped into place. Separate longitudinals that incorporate the side windows' upper seals complete the top, which stows in a fitted leather bag in the front-mounted trunk when not in use. Top up, a sign on the windshield header reminds you not to drive the car over 100 mph (I picture an F-16 jettisoning its canopy as the pilot punches out—and fasten my seatbelt!).

The arrival of the Gallardo in 2003, and the horsepower arms race that subsequently kicked off with Ferrari, impinged somewhat on the Murciélago's territory. The original Gallardo's V-10 made a claimed 500 PS (493 brake horsepower), not too far off the Murciélago V-12's claimed 580 PS (572 brake horsepower), and in power-to-weight terms the performance gap was narrower still. When Ferrari deployed the F430, prompting Lamborghini to spruce up the Gallardo's performance for its 2005 refresh, the "baby Lambo" crossed the Rubicon: 520 PS (513 brake horsepower). And a second-generation model that would be more powerful still was in the works.

To that end, for 2006 the Murciélago also gained a performance boost in a midlife rebirth aimed at putting clear water between it and its junior sibling. While the exterior changes amounted to little more than a mild sharpening of the lines around the nose and tail, there were plenty of changes under the skin. The occupant of the engine bay was stretched to 6.5 liters and given a new variable valve-timing system, bringing power to a claimed 640 PS (631 brake horsepower)—hence the new LP640 badging—though it exhaled through a new exhaust system that left some observers nonplussed.

"It muffles the V12's voice to the point that you wonder if you've gone partially deaf," wrote *Evo* magazine's John Barker. "Proof that you haven't is there in the shape of the multiple warning bongs and chimes that almost drown out the aurally castrated V12—door open, key in ignition, seatbelt undone, shirt not buttoned-up properly. . . ."

In reprogramming the paddle-shift gearbox and upgrading the clutch, Lamborghini also implemented a so-called safety measure that prevented the driver from engaging a gear while one of the doors was open. This made it impossible to reverse "Balboni-style," an out-of-the-seat parking technique perfected by test driver Valentino Balboni and imitated badly by many owners. On the move, though, the new Murciélago LP640 confounded expectations that it had gone all politically correct.

"It's a relief to find that from the driver's seat the Murciélago's character and appeal remain intact," noted Barker. "Inside, the sound of the engine's exertions is largely undiminished, and the big V12 remains a mighty, energetic, and stimulating force at your back, climbing to its red line with an epic, ever-changing soundscape that finally hardens and resolves for the stomach-flipping lunge to the limiter. The Gallardo's V10 is a fine engine, but an extra pair of cylinders makes a big difference."

Lamborghini only partially addressed the first-gen Murciélago's poor braking performance, adding carbon-ceramic anchors to the options list (alongside, among other things, a glass engine cover) at a rather steep $12,500. For the keen driver another headline change to the spec, a new Kenwood stereo system, seemed superfluous, though the new bucket seats were an improvement. It was disappointing, too, to see other ergonomic quirks, such as the slightly offset instrument binnacle, go unimproved.

There was also a growing feeling that the Murciélago's steel-frame underpinnings were antediluvian in comparison with lighter, more nimble rivals that were appearing with composite monocoques. "The Murciélago undisputedly still remains relevant, or as relevant as a 212mph 1.7-tonne two-seat lorry can be," wrote Chris Chilton in *Car* magazine after testing a new LP640.

The car's old-school structure did open up the potential for it to be adapted to run in GT racing, though, with the possibility of establishing a profitable sideline in supplying these variants to customers. German tuner Reiter Engineering developed a rear-wheel-drive-only version of the Murciélago designated the R-GT, but GT racing in the 2000s was a fickle environment of proliferating series, and beset by arguments over how the performance of very different cars could be balanced. Only a handful of R-GTs were built, although one won the opening race of the 2007 FIA GT Championship.

Murciélago LP640

Chassis	Tubular steel monocoque with composite inserts
Suspension	Independent double wishbones front/rear, coaxial coil springs, telescopic self-adjusting shock absorbers, anti-roll bars, and anti-squat bars
Brakes	Ventilated Brembo discs with ABS and DRP (carbon-ceramic optional)
Wheelbase	2665 mm
Front/rear track	1635 mm/1695 mm
Wheels/Tires	18 in × 8.5 in, Pirelli PZero 245/35 (front); 18 in × 13 in, Pirelli PZero 335/30 (rear)
Engine	Rear longitudinal-mounted 60-degree V-12
Bore/Stroke	88 mm/89 mm
Cubic capacity	6496 cc
Compression ratio	11.0:1
Maximum power	631 bhp at 8000 rpm
Valve gear	Dual overhead camshafts, chain drive, 4 valves per cylinder, continuously variable timing
Fuel/ignition system	Lamborghini electronic fuel injection, individual coils
Lubrication	Dry sump
Gearbox	Lamborghini 6-speed manual (e-gear robotized manual optional)
Transmission	Four-wheel drive
Clutch	Dry single-plate
Dry weight	1650 kg (Roadster 1665 kg)
Top speed	211 mph (Roadster 205 mph)

Lamborghini continued to refresh the Murciélago, following up the anniversary edition in 2006 with a run of 20 coupes and roadsters custom-trimmed in collaboration with the Versace fashion house. Each car arrived with matching Versace luggage and driving accessories.

In 2009, with the end of the line in sight and development of the Aventador underway, the most extreme variant yet of the Murciélago made its debut. The LP670-4 SuperVeloce's name was an implicit nod to a badging history that stretched back to the Miura, and there was no mistaking it for an "ordinary" Murciélago if you selected the optional "Aeropack," which featured a prominent racing-style spoiler at the rear, at a cost of losing three miles per hour from the top speed (somewhat academic, since the quoted top speed sans wing was 212 miles per hour).

"Despite sacrificing top speed," wrote Car and Driver's Gregory Anderson, "serious drivers will opt for the Aeropack because the big fixed wing creates so much downforce that Lamborghini should consider changing the name to SG, for Super Glue. On the 16-turn, 3.9-mile handling track at the Nardò proving ground in southern Italy, the SV's rear end always remained firmly planted, in contrast to the base Murciélago's occasional booty shake around tight corners."

Although engine power rose to 670 PS (661 brake horsepower), the SV's trump card came in the form of a claimed 220-pound weight loss program, attributed to a more thorough use of carbon fiber and lightweight steel in the chassis, a lighter exhaust system, a fixed rear spoiler (thus eliminating the weight of the motors for the moveable one), and infuriatingly unyielding carbon-shelled seats. Road & Track achieved 0–60 miles per hour in 2.8 seconds during performance testing on the runway of a former airbase. That's a full second faster than the first-generation model.

To complement the lighter weight, Lamborghini tuned the steering to make it feel sharper. Ferrari had just launched the HGTE handling pack of its 599 model, to which the LP670-4 SV came as a brutal riposte. Wrote David Vivian in Evo:

> It isn't just the accelerative lunge for the horizon that momentarily makes me forget to breathe, but the way it builds to a shattering crescendo gear after gear. In summary, this thing goes like hell.

And corners do little to blunt its charge. What's perhaps most remarkable about the SV's chassis is its eagerness to translate even the most fleeting and subtle helm input into meaningful action. You can nuance a cornering line with steering or throttle. And with so much width to place on the road, it's a revelation that it can be done so accurately. This is the other side to the SV's character—it feels focused and intimate. The colossal output from the engine is met without contrivance or nerves from the chassis. Just grip, conviction and precision.

Power oversteer? With the torque split rear-biased it isn't off the agenda, especially if you stay on the brakes while turning in, but you'd better be quick with the opposite lock. Let it get too out of shape and there's no way back.

As sales of the Murciélago began to tail off—a combination of the global recession and wealthy prospects keeping their wallets in their pockets in anticipation of the car's replacement—Lamborghini sought to feed interest with a final pair of limited-edition models. The LP 670-4 SuperVeloce China Limited Edition of 2010 drew attention largely because of its supersized moniker; 10 were built, aimed, as the name rendered explicit, for the Chinese market, and were no different from the standard SV save for the color, which was gloss gray with a central black-and-orange stripe. Lamborghini claimed the stripe was chosen to "symbolize the strength of an erupting volcano"—unfortunate, given that many of the foreign delegates at the Beijing show, where the car was unveiled, were unable to fly home because of the ash cloud from the eruption of Eyjafjallajökull in Iceland.

Less niche was the LP650-4 Roadster, a 20-model run of the roofless Murciélago with two-tone paintwork, in Grigio Telesto with Arancia detailing, and a two-tone interior with different shades of black leather and alcantara for the driver and passenger side. To differentiate it from the work of custom painters, Lamborghini liberated a little more power from the engine to give 650 PS (641 brake horsepower), thus rendering it suitably exclusive.

The LP670-4 SV was certainly among the most viscerally exciting cars ever to take to the road, but, launched into a market that had been chilled by recession, it would fail to sell in the numbers anticipated. Lambo claimed that 350 would be built before the production line was dismantled to make way for the Aventador. In reality, the number of SVs made and sold barely reached half that figure.

In spite of this muted coda, the Murciélago was an incredible success. Nine years after that intensely flamboyant launch, production of the car that relaunched Lamborghini and defined the brand's destination in the 21st century came to an end. On November 5, 2010, accompanied by a respectful ceremonial send-off featuring an escort from a police Gallardo, a 350GT, a Miura, a Countach, a Diablo, and a white LP670-4 SV, Murciélago number 4,099—an SV painted in Arancio Atlas—rolled off the line. It had taken 11 years to sell 2,903 Diablos.

Murciélago LP670-4 SuperVeloce

Chassis	Tubular steel monocoque with composite inserts
Suspension	Independent double wishbones front/rear, coaxial coil springs, telescopic self-adjusting shock absorbers, anti-roll bars, and anti-squat bars
Brakes	Ventilated carbon-ceramic Brembo discs with ABS and DRP
Wheelbase	2665 mm
Front/rear track	1635 mm/1695 mm
Wheels/Tires	18 in × 8.5 in, Pirelli PZero 245/35 (front); 18 in × 13 in, Pirelli PZero 335/30 (rear)
Engine	Rear longitudinal-mounted 60-degree V-12
Bore/Stroke	88 mm/89 mm
Cubic capacity	6496 cc
Compression ratio	11.0:1
Maximum power	661 bhp at 8000 rpm
Valve gear	Dual overhead camshafts, chain drive, 4 valves per cylinder, continuously variable timing
Fuel/ignition system	Lamborghini electronic fuel injection, individual coils
Lubrication	Dry sump
Gearbox	Lamborghini 6-speed e-gear robotized manual
Transmission	Four-wheel drive
Clutch	Dry single-plate
Dry weight	1565 kg
Top speed	213 mph

GALLARDO

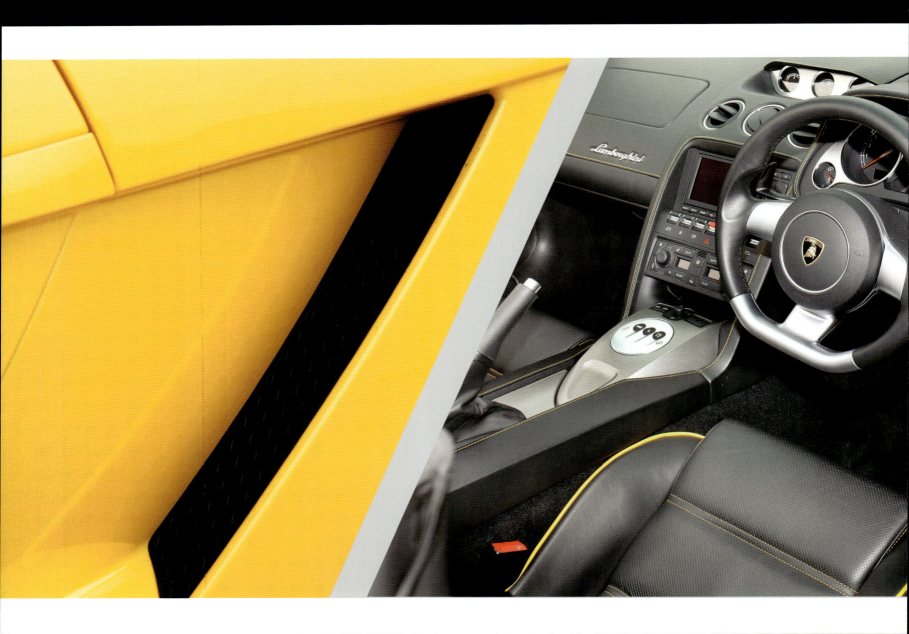

THIS WAS A HIGH-STAKES GAME. When Audi collected the keys of the Sant'Agata factory in July 1998, its senior management knew that all eyes would be on the successor to Lamborghini's marquee car, the Diablo. But not for long. Audi had done its sums diligently and come to the conclusion that Lamborghini needed to shift 1,500 cars a year minimum to stay afloat. It had not come anywhere near that, ever; hence, the procession of different owners, each departing amid the jetsam of thwarted ambition. It needed a more accessible and affordable model, a successor to the Jalpa, but preferably one that would actually sell.

THE DRIVER'S SUPERCAR

Getting the Murciélago off the ground to replace the aging Diablo was the priority, but within 18 months of the buyout Audi started to factor the so-called "baby Diablo" into its thinking. To lighten the load on chief designer Luc Donkerwolke's embryonic Lamborghini Centro Stile, in early 2000 Audi invited styling proposals from its own in-house design team as well as Italian coachbuilders Italdesign, Bertone, and IDEA. Italdesign already had something ready to go, designed several years earlier by Fabrizio Giugiaro, son of Giorgetto.

At the Geneva show in 1995, Italdesign had demonstrated a 2+2 "research prototype" called the Calà, openly acknowledging the influence of the Lamborghini Miura and Countach on some of its design elements. Beneath the composite skin was an aluminum chassis. Show-goers were accustomed to Italian design houses indulging in blue-sky whimsy, so many were inclined to mosey on past without asking too many questions. A few, unkindly, were moved by the rather unbalanced look of the air scoops on its shoulders to comment that Fabrizio Giugiaro had some way to go before emulating his father. Mechanically, though, the Calà was worth a second look: not only was the drivetrain Lamborghini-based, with a Sant'Agata four-liter 372-brake-horsepower V-10 engine (built in the Chrysler era) driving the rear wheels, but the car itself was perfectly drivable. No simple styling mule, this.

The Calà would never see production in its original form, but Italdesign revisited the idea when invited to create a styling proposal for the car that would become the Gallardo; and what had been left to wither on the vine for lack of investment by Megatech in 1995 would, just a few years later, become the foundation of Audi's grand plan to make Lamborghini a financially viable concern.

Only the Audi and Italdesign proposals went through to the final phase, with the updated Calà getting the nod. So too did the aluminum spaceframe concept, although as development progressed the senior engineering team suddenly applied the brakes: the car needed to be more compact. This would involve a major re-skin of the body, overseen by Donckerwolke. He tightened the design, harmonizing some elements with the forthcoming Murciélago, changing the round taillamps for wrap-over ones, reshaping the headlights and air intakes, and specifying a movable rear spoiler that only manifested itself at speed. The finished car was reckoned to be 70 percent Donckerwolke, 30 percent Italdesign.

Since the Gallardo would be going in to bat against established opposition, chiefly the V-8-engined Ferrari 360 Modena and the flat-six Porsche 911, getting the powertrain and driving experience right was arguably more important than nailing the look. There could be no excuses for wayward handling, slack quality control, offset driver contact points, or switchgear sited as if fired at the styling buck with a blunderbuss.

The extant four-liter V-10 engine was too small and packed insufficient wallop to pass muster in the 21st century; but the engineering team thought a V-8 would be rather "me too," certainly not enough to up the ante against Ferrari. So a five-liter V-10 it would be, albeit one based on the architecture of an existing Audi V-8 (see "V-10

Although the Gallardo was produced on a highly automated line, in greater numbers than any previous Lamborghini, much of the detail work was done by hand.

power"]. Once news of this leaked out, it set the grapevine humming: was this the thin end of the dumbing-down wedge for Lamborghini?

Cassandras need not have applied. "You're going to love it," wrote *Autocar*'s venerable European editor, Peter Robinson, after a trip to Sant'Agata in May 2003. "The Gallardo's deep roar couldn't be more different from the high-frequency shriek of the flat-crank V8 in Ferrari's 360 Modena, or the natural bellow of the Murciélago's V12. Nor is it at all like the subdued mechanical noise of the Audi V8 from which the V10 is circuitously derived."

Packaging dictated the engine's racing-style *V* angle. "We looked at a 72-degree V10," said chief engineer Massimo Ceccarani. "But the centre of gravity would have been higher and the packaging compromised. Obviously we made some synergies [with the Audi V-8] but it all started out from the concept of a 90-degree V10."

Take that, Porsche and Ferrari; at launch the Gallardo's V-10 delivered a peak output of 493 brake horsepower, compared with the 911's 414 brake horsepower and the 360 Modena's 394 brake horsepower. As word got around, the dyno jockeys of Maranello and Stuttgart began to sharpen their pencils.

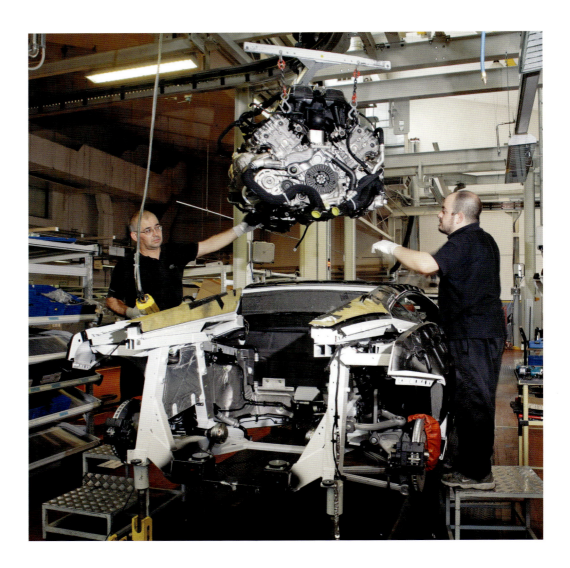

Manufacture of the Gallardo's mighty V-10 was outsourced to other companies in the Audi group, with final assembly happening in Hungary before the complete units were shipped to Sant'Agata.

Since the factory was still under development—a museum and admin block was added in 2001, and the Gallardo production line was installed over the winter of 2002–2003—many elements of the Gallardo were outsourced. The aluminum spaceframes were fabricated in Germany by Krupp-Drauz and then painted at an Audi facility, the former NSU plant at Neckarsulm, before being shipped overland to Sant'Agata for assembly on the new line.

The Gallardo's suspension wishbones were also aluminum, and it was the first production car within the Audi group to use Koni's Frequency Selective damping system, a passive technology that progressively adjusted the damper settings according to the road conditions. Below a certain degree of jiggle they were set to their hardest, then once vertical movement exceeded 7 hz an internal valve would open to soften the damping and rebound.

The year 2003 would be crunch time for Lamborghini. The Gallardo assembly line was completed in February, the car unveiled at Geneva in March, and then dealers and media were selectively introduced to it in April through June. Lamborghini's dealer network bit in a big way; its US network alone ordered 35 percent of the Gallardos to be built that year, projected to be 890 units. Soon the factory was working double shifts to ensure that demand was met.

Next up, the media. The drip-feed began with a group of five journalists driving a stealth-black pre-production Gallardo around Italy's Imola circuit in late May. *Autocar*'s Robinson was among them:

> Although it feels rather more spacious than—dare I say—the bigger Murciélago, and Audi's influence is apparent in the superior ergonomics and use of the same climate and sound system that you'll find in an A4, the cockpit's genes are strictly Lamborghini.
>
> The base of the windscreen is so far forward that it's in front of the end of my feet. From here, slumped down low, it's hard to believe there's any bonnet at all. The pillars, rising out of the top of the front wheel arches, are thick and fast of angle—to the obvious detriment of visibility. The view over the shoulder, hindered by the buttresses from the roof almost to the very end of the car, remains true to Sant'Agata's who-cares-what's-behind-you attitude. So flat and cab-forward is the windscreen that the exterior mirrors are mounted on front-facing arms that emerge from the doors.

Undoubtedly a Lamborghini, then, but with most of the ergonomic rough edges smoothed off. As for those that remained—well, a wedgy, low-slung supercar was never going to afford its occupants the same commanding view as a minivan, was it? The only disappointment one might have voiced was the absence of scissor doors, but this, it's believed, was a deliberate choice by Lamborghini to establish boundaries between the Gallardo and the more exclusive Murciélago.

Regardless of its performance compared with its rivals, the Gallardo had incredible spectator appeal. As Aaron Robinson noted in *Car and Driver*:

> Who really cares what side of the Alps the pieces come from as you strafe the freeways in a Lamborghini Gallardo? Certainly not the other commuters, their noses pancaked to the glass and their ears twitching with each 493 bhp whoop from the V-10 wailing at your shoulder blades.
>
> Even the starter motor on the Gallardo sounds fast. Turn the key, and the frenetic chugging ends in a sultry whoosh of combustion as the 303-cubic-inch DOHC 40-valve V-10 ignites. The engine settles quickly on a breathless 1000-rpm idle, ready for anything from a lazy trawl down a boulevard to a blast up to the 8100-rpm redline, the wide torque band pushing hard from rest and the intake tract sucking obscenely from the fender ducts.

Glitches with the e-gear robotized manual gearbox, a development of a Magnetti Marelli system also used by Ferrari, Maserati, and Aston Martin, frustrated early attempts to run back-to-back performance tests between the Gallardo and its closest rivals. It, and associated excessive clutch wear, would continue to be a bugbear with owners, especially those who made frequent use of "thrust mode"—an automatic flying start system that optimized getaways from a standing start with a controlled amount of wheelspin. But the alternative transmission—a six-speed manual gearbox with overly long and springy clutch action and a slow, clunky throw—was equally disagreeable.

Nevertheless, in late October 2004 Ferrari launched its 360 Modena replacement, the F430, 18 months earlier than expected—a clear sign that the Gallardo was considered a serious contender. The F430 occupied the same price bracket, was 70 kilograms lighter (thanks to the absence of four-wheel drive), and only a shade less powerful at 483 brake horsepower. Ferrari, as usual, organized its press car schedule to thwart direct comparisons, but by subterfuge *Autocar* pulled off the trick. The ensuing test proved a very close call, with fine margins.

"The Gallardo's steering is weighty and accurate," wrote Ben Oliver, "but its responses feel programmed rather than natural and the rim lifeless after the light but fizzy Ferrari rack. The slight torque response that corrupts the four-wheel-drive Gallardo's steering in tighter bends is absent in the Ferrari, as is the mild understeer . . . and when the engines are working at the top of the range the Ferrari's slight power-to-weight advantage seems to count double; the throttle response more urgent, the kick in the backside even harder. Am I really about to write that a near-500bhp Lamborghini feels slow? After the deft, light, frenetic Ferrari, it does; it's slower and slightly wooden."

Lamborghini's riposte came within months in the form of a 250-model limited-edition SE, each individually numbered, with a two-tone color scheme (including a choice of six different main shades) and new wheel rims, along with trim changes and more standard equipment, such as a rear-facing camera to facilitate parking. It also had a different steering rack, promised to sharpen the steering response, and shorter ratios in the first five gears. The technical changes, plus revised engine mapping (giving 513 brake horsepower) and a rortier exhaust, were rolled out to the rest of the range for the 2006 model year. The tweaked car also featured a lifting mechanism at the front to temporarily increase ground clearance by four inches when negotiating urban obstacles such as speed bumps; it worked by feeding extra oil, driven by the power steering pump, into the front shock absorbers.

Lamborghini wasn't done improving the first-generation Gallardo, launching a Spyder open-top variant at the 2006 Los Angeles show and then putting the coupe on a crash diet for a special model to be unveiled at Geneva in March 2007. The Superleggera's name was a play on the lightweight construction method patented in the 1930s by the long-defunct Carrozzeria Touring, Lamborghini's coachbuilder of choice in the marque's early years.

To achieve a 100-kilogram weight reduction (70 kilograms in cars for the US market), Lamborghini swapped out many metal components for carbon fiber and polycarbonate. The engine hood, the rear diffuser, door panels, and mirrors, along with various pieces of interior trim—including the seats—all received this treatment. The

Gallardo Spyder

glasshouse—with the exception of the windscreen—was replaced with transparent polycarbonate. Detail changes to the intake and exhaust manifolds to aid volumetric efficiency, plus a reprogrammed ECU, brought power to a claimed 523 brake horsepower; it could complete the 0–62 miles per hour benchmark acceleration test in 3.8 seconds, two-tenths of a second faster than the standard model. A sportier suspension package, previously optional on Gallardos, was now standard, as was the e-gear transmission. You could have a Gallardo Superleggera in four colors: Telesto Gray, Noctis Black, Borealis Orange, and Midas Yellow.

A disorderly queue formed to drive it. *Autocar* test driver Steve Sutcliffe, a racer of note in the ultra-hairy TVR Tuscan Challenge, wrote:

> The noise is what hits you first, because the Superleggera's new exhaust system has liberated a good few extra decibels from the V10, especially at the top end. But the real step forward is the handling; it is now close to racing-car sharp, and although the steering is meatier than before, the way the Superleggera hangs on through quick corners, and changes direction so rapidly through slower bends, is enough to make the back of your neck go all tingly. The brakes, too, are monumental once the (optional) carbon ceramic discs have come up to temperature.

Gallardo

Chassis	Aluminum spaceframe
Suspension	Independent double wishbones front/rear, coaxial coil springs, telescopic self-adjusting shock absorbers, anti-roll bars, and anti-squat bars
Brakes	Ventilated Brembo discs with ABS, ASR, and ABD
Wheelbase	2560 mm
Front/rear track	1592 mm/1622 mm
Wheels/Tires	19 in × 8.5 in, Pirelli PZero 235/35 (front); 19 in × 11 in, Pirelli PZero 295/30 (rear)
Engine	Rear longitudinal-mounted 90-degree V-10
Bore/Stroke	82.5 mm/92.8 mm
Cubic capacity	4961 cc
Compression ratio	11.0:1
Maximum power	493 bhp at 7800 rpm (513 bhp from 2006 model year)
Valve gear	Dual overhead camshafts, chain drive, 4 valves per cylinder, continuously variable timing
Fuel/ignition system	Lamborghini electronic fuel injection, individual coils
Lubrication	Dry sump
Gearbox	Lamborghini 6-speed manual (e-gear robotized manual optional)
Transmission	Four-wheel drive
Clutch	Dry single-plate
Dry weight	1430 kg (Spyder 1570 kg)
Top speed	196 mph (Spyder 195 mph)

The only downside is what the Superleggera does on or near the limit of its admittedly huge reserves of grip. Thanks to standard-fit Pirelli P-Zero Corsa tyres, adhesion in the dry is enough to make your eyes water, and even when you press on hard the underlying trait is understeer. But if you do end up having to deal with an oversteer slide, you need to be lightning-quick with your inputs to avoid a spin. Gone, in other words, is the creamy, benign on-limit balance of the regular car. And that's the price you pay, inevitably, for having so much grip up to the point of no return.

The mainstream Gallardo model urgently needed to get back in the game though, so at the Geneva show in 2008 Lamborghini unveiled the second-generation model, boasting a Reventón-esque facelift around the mouth and, more importantly, an all-new 5.2-liter direct injection V-10 engine just aft of the driver and a lower dry weight. Badged LP560-4 in line with Lambo's new style of model nomenclature, highlighting (metric) power output and the number of driven wheels along with the location and alignment of the engine, the new Gallardo was a clear improvement on the outgoing model.

Although the exterior changes were mild, they were claimed to improve aerodynamic efficiency and meet pedestrian impact regulations that had yet to come into force. Front and rear LED daytime running lights were in line with Audi's flagship models, giving the car an additional note of purpose as it grew larger in the rearview mirrors of the driver in front. The whole back end was also mildly restyled with a more integrated look, including a new diffuser claimed to improve high-speed stability. The passenger compartment was also given a lift, with a new instrument binnacle and dual-zone air conditioning, and it was extensively customizable under Lamborghini's new Ad Personam program.

There was also the promise of an improved, lighter, faster-shifting e-gear system, now offering five driver-selectable shift modes that also unlocked different power delivery characteristics via the engine ECU. In the track-focused Corsa mode, the shift time had been reduced by 40 percent, but this, as owners would find out, came at a cost of a particularly abrupt transition.

A Spyder variant soon followed, and with good reason. "Lamborghini says that the Spyder version of its Gallardo outsells the Coupé variant almost two to one," wrote *Top Gear*'s Tom Ford with a barely concealed sneer. "Which underlines a fact that we all probably suspected: Lamborghini owners really like to show off. Subtlety not required, ability to attract Russian prostitutes with nothing more than a lazy drive-by, an absolute selling point."

Over successive years Lamborghini added further breadth to the range, adding a Superleggera version of the second-generation model, badged LP570-4 to highlight its modest power bump, followed by an open-top version called the Spyder Performante. It also added a two-wheel-drive variant to function as an entry-level model, the LP550-2, allegedly to honor the retirement of longtime chief test driver Valentino Balboni, whose preference was for the purity of rear-wheel drive. A limited-run (250 models) "Balboni" special edition followed, distinguished by a center stripe with a gold border; though not as rare as, say, the Reventón, this model has acquired cult status among Lamborghini aficionados.

Following the successful launch of the Aventador, the Gallardo was treated to a facelift for its final year of manufacture, 2013. In essence this amounted to a pair of diagonal bars across the air intakes front and rear, along with alloy wheels finished in black with silver highlights, as was fashionable at the time. Potential owners wanting a final touch that was a little unusual, without being vulgar, could avail themselves of an optional styling package in which various pieces of exterior bodywork finished in matte black as standard were repainted in high gloss.

In November 2013 Lamborghini management and factory staff attended a small ceremony to mark a significant moment: the last Gallardo off the production line, an LP570-4 Spyder Performante, the 14,022nd Gallardo to be built. Cars such as the Miura created the Lamborghini legend, but the Gallardo—by a substantial margin the marque's most successful car ever until the Urus surpassed it—gave that legend longevity.

Gallardo LP560-4

Chassis	Aluminum spaceframe
Suspension	Independent double wishbones front/rear, coaxial coil springs, telescopic self-adjusting shock absorbers, anti-roll bars, and anti-squat bars
Brakes	Ventilated Brembo discs with ABS, ASR, and ABD
Wheelbase	2560 mm
Front/rear track	1597 mm/1632 mm
Wheels/Tires	19 in × 8.5 in, Pirelli PZero 235/35 (front); 19 in × 11 in, Pirelli PZero 295/30 (rear)
Engine	Rear longitudinal-mounted 90-degree V-10
Bore/Stroke	84.5 mm/92.8 mm
Cubic capacity	5204 cc
Compression ratio	11.0:1
Maximum power	552 bhp at 8000 rpm (LP570-4 562 bhp)
Valve gear	Dual overhead camshafts, chain drive, 4 valves per cylinder, continuously variable timing
Fuel/ignition system	Bosch electronically controlled direct injection, individual coils
Lubrication	Dry sump
Gearbox	Lamborghini 6-speed manual (e-gear robotized manual optional)
Transmission	Four-wheel drive
Clutch	Dry single-plate
Dry weight	1500 kg (Spyder 1570 kg)
Top speed	202 mph (Spyder 201 mph)

V-10 POWER

Lamborghini already had a V-10 engine developed in the mid-1990s, but when this was deemed unsuitable by Audi, an all-new unit had to be developed in double-quick time. To achieve this, Lamborghini based the architecture of the dry-sumped block on that of Audi's extant 4.2-liter V-8 and combined it with newly designed pistons and conrods, adding new four-valve cylinder heads created in consultation with Cosworth Technology.

Cosworth is a familiar name to motor racing fans. The VW Group acquired it from defense manufacturer Vickers in 1998 and sold the racing division to Ford, retaining its casting and engineering facilities. The first Lamborghini V-10s started life in Cosworth Technology's foundry in Worcester, UK, before being shipped to another Audi facility in Hungary for fit-out, then sent on to Sant'Agata as mostly finished units.

Although this engine earned plaudits from critics and owners, it had a remarkably short shelf life for a modern powertrain. Not that it was a conspicuous weak spot of the car—early criticisms focused on build quality problems and the refinement of the gear shift, along with unusually high clutch wear. The problem was that Ferrari didn't welcome this invasion of its turf and fired back by improving its own models. For the 2006 model year Lamborghini revised the exhaust system, consolidating what had previously been two separate mufflers into one and engineering a pair of bypass valves that kept noise low while trickling around urban areas but added volume when the driver put pedal to metal.

A glance at the specifications of the 5.2-liter V-10 powering the second-generation Gallardo model, launched in 2008, might lead you to conclude that it's the original but with two-millimeter wider bores. In fact, the block was a new design, with wider bore centers and a longer crankshaft that was also stiffer and stronger to counter vibration problems experienced with the original engine.

"The old engine was at the limit of its power and capacity," technical director Maurizio Reggiani explained at the revised Gallardo's unveiling at the Geneva show in 2008.

Where the first V-10 maintained an even firing interval of 72 degrees, using split crankpins between opposing cylinders, in the new engine Lamborghini used common pins to give firing intervals of 90 degrees and 58 degrees. This, together with a new exhaust system, completely transformed the soundtrack, especially under hard acceleration.

Adopting Audi's Fuel Stratified Injection system (it sounds better in Italian: Iniezione Diretta Stratificata) gave better combustion characteristics, including reduced sensitivity to knock, which allowed a greater compression ratio of 12.5:1. This helped boost power as well as reducing CO_2 emissions by 18 percent. The latter improvement was perhaps located some way south of power, noise, and feel on the priority list of most owners.

"Fire up the Lambo and you might think it's powered by a whole other V10," wrote *Evo* magazine's John Barker in a back-to-back comparison test with Audi's R8 when that car became available with the Lambo V10, albeit in 34 brake horsepower milder tune. "It catches with a thunderous outburst loaded with a fluty, off-beat yowl, and if there are valves in its exhaust system they appear to be jammed open. It's hungry, edgy sounding at all times, and it behaves how it sounds. The R8 has superb throttle response but the Gallardo snaps forward like it's been given an electric shock, and the force that drives you into your seat is stronger too."

RACING THE GALLARDO

Lamborghinis have been prepared for and entered in various GT race series over the years, but the factory itself always adhered to Ferruccio Lamborghini's tenet that racing was a mug's game unless you were winning. But, as Enzo Ferrari had proved, selling race cars could be a profitable business. So as Lamborghini expanded its reach under Audi's leadership, hungry for sales, racing came on the agenda once again.

German tuner Reiter Engineering had prepared racing Murciélagos for private clients including the Japanese Lamborghini Owners Club, and some two-wheel-drive Gallardos for the Japanese SuperGT series. Through 2008 the company was called upon to develop a new version of the Gallardo for a one-make race series along the lines of the long defunct Lamborghini Super Trophy. The championship, called the Lamborghini Blancpain Super Trofeo, would run on the support card of major international series including FIA GT, Formula 3, and the DTM, and pair wealthy amateur drivers with seasoned professionals in a multi-race pro-am format at a cost of €200,000.

Owing to the effects of the global recession, initial uptake was slow and the first event—due to support the FIA GT series at Silverstone in May 2009—was canceled. But the organizers pulled enough entries together for the series to kick off at Adria Raceway a few weeks later with a 15-car grid (30 had been built).

Reiter stripped 110 kilograms from the car and beefed up the suspension to cope with the rigors of racing. To make it friendlier for the less experienced gentlemen racers, they retained the all-wheel drive, but with a lightweight exhaust system and revisions to the engine management that liberated some more horsepower, bringing the total to 570 PS (562 brake horsepower).

Other racing addenda included a carbon fiber bodykit, and the glasshouse was replaced with polycarbonate. For reasons that must have seemed eminently plausible at the time, the brakes were steel—and, though the car had been through a number of preseason tests, actual racing exposed this as a weak point. A weekend featuring three 40-minute races was enough to toast the brakes in most cars.

Subsequent revisions ameliorated the brake problems, and in spite of a few other teething troubles the series found its legs and expanded into the US and Asia. In 2011 Lamborghini took race car manufacture and organization in-house under a new department, Squadra Corsa. Gallardos also continued to race in GT3 specification in GT series worldwide.

Gallardo LP550-2

Chassis	Aluminum spaceframe
Suspension	Independent double wishbones front/rear, coaxial coil springs, telescopic self-adjusting shock absorbers, anti-roll bars, and anti-squat bars
Brakes	Ventilated Brembo discs with ABS, ASR, and ABD
Wheelbase	2560 mm
Front/rear track	1597 mm/1632 mm
Wheels/Tires	19 in × 8.5 in, Pirelli PZero 235/35 (front); 19 in × 11 in, Pirelli PZero 295/30 (rear)
Engine	Rear longitudinal-mounted 90-degree V-10
Bore/Stroke	84.5 mm/92.8 mm
Cubic capacity	5204 cc
Compression ratio	11.0:1
Maximum power	542 bhp at 8000 rpm
Valve gear	Dual overhead camshafts, chain drive, 4 valves per cylinder, continuously variable timing
Fuel/ignition system	Bosch electronically controlled direct injection, individual coils
Lubrication	Dry sump
Gearbox	Lamborghini 6-speed manual (e-gear robotized manual optional)
Transmission	Two-wheel drive
Clutch	Dry single-plate
Dry weight	1380 kg (Spyder 1520 kg)
Top speed	199 mph (Spyder 198 mph)

REVENTÓN

TEN YEARS AFTER AUDI BOUGHT LAMBORGHINI, and as the Murciélago reached middle age, the next phase of the corporate strategy came on stream: establishing a profitable sideline in manufacturing boutique exotica for the super wealthy. Was there any compelling need to develop a more extreme iteration of the Murciélago? Probably not—but, to paraphrase John F. Kennedy's famous speech announcing his intention to put a man on the moon, it was a goal that served to organize and measure the best of Lamborghini's energies and skills as it sought to establish its brand values in the 21st century.

EXCLUSIVE PERFORMANCE

Road & Track echoed these sentiments but couched them slightly differently: "Deciding not to wait until a coachbuilder picks up a Murciélago to convert it into something different, Lamborghini decided it could do the job better and started work on project code LP640/2, aka the M.O.A., which stands for 'Meanest of All.' Spokesman Dominik Hoberg said the designation was decided on because the car is expected to have 'at least' 650 bhp."

But although the Reventón was named after a Miura bull that killed bullfighter Félix Guzman in 1943, it was no more lethal than the Murciélago with which it shared underpinnings. While its engine was blueprinted to liberate an extra 10 brake horsepower, and much of the bodywork was composite, the Reventón was nowhere near as extreme as the Gallardo Superleggera, as chairman and CEO Stephan Winkelmann explained: "Our designers at the Lamborghini Centro Stile based in Sant'Agata took the technical base of the Murciélago LP640 and compressed and intensified its DNA, its genetic code."

Still stuck? Peruse the press materials, which were sprinkled with terms such as "haute couture." Or go straight to the VW Group horse's mouth; in its 2007 annual report it said, "The idea behind this strictly limited edition of 20 vehicles was to create a model that would crown the success of the brand, that will serve as a four-wheeled ambassador for the uniqueness of Lamborghini—and that will also demonstrate the short development times of which the sports car manufacturer is now capable."

In effect, Lamborghini took a car that few would describe as common—unless they lived in certain areas of London or Dubai—and made it super exclusive. Its exterior

Reventón Roadster

dressing was just that—a different and more rarefied set of clothes for a set of preferred customers Lamborghini defined as "friends and collectors." Only 20 would ever be built. The driving experience was largely unchanged, the handling no better, the acceleration broadly similar.

But what a set of clothes this was. The sharp creases and strakes, along with the proportions on the glasshouse, were reportedly inspired by the F-22 Raptor airplane—territory Lamborghini's designers would return to again and again over the coming years. To complete the Area 51 effect, each Reventón was finished in a shade Lamborghini waxed lyrical over: "Naturally, such a refined language of shape also demands an extraordinary color. For the 20 examples of the Reventón, the designers from Sant'Agata Bolognese have created a totally new hue: Reventón, a mid opaque green/grey without the usual shine."

A car hack looking for a cheap punchline would "uh-huh" at this hyperbole and describe the actual color as a matte gray. But seen in real life, up close, the stealth paintwork possesses a subtle shimmer thanks to the many thousands of tiny metallic particles in the mix. Lamborghini would do this again, to pleasing effect, with the Sesto Elemento.

The jet fighter cues ran from the sharp, pointy nose with its aggressive brake-cooling ducts (the six-pot calipers grasping carbon discs) through to the prominent rear diffuser and adjustable rear wing. The air intakes below the doors were asymmetrical, the one on the driver's side being larger in order to direct air to the radiator. With just one nod to style over function, the glass composite engine cover's open ventilation slots offered a view of the V-12 bellowing beneath—like that of the original Miura, only more coherently resolved with the rest of the car.

The composite panels were riveted and bonded to the chassis, as they were on the Murciélago, crowned with a billeted aluminum fuel cap and LED taillights. Inside, the driver had the option to switch the LCD fascia display between a traditional dial effect and something resembling a fighter jet's heads-up display—it even featured an airplane-style g-force meter that gave continuous indication of the intensity and direction of the forces acting on the car. Tellingly, the Reventón was only offered with the e-gear transmission, a clear pointer to future models dropping the manual shift option.

Since just 20 models were to be offered to customers, the Reventón rapidly acquired an almost mythic status. The Lamborghini Blancpain Super Trofeo race series (see page 146) might have been a mere support act for more prestigious international championships, but Lambo's lavish "hospitality village" for drivers and VIPs, artfully dressed as a sort of military enclosure (complete with camouflage canvas) proved to be a massive draw for spectators. Part of that allure can be put down to the curb appeal of the Reventón that formed part of the display; it looked like a parked UFO.

Select media were allowed to drive a pre-production car. "It's a show-stopper," wrote *Autocar*'s Michael Taylor. "A normal Murciélago will stop traffic and turn heads. A Reventón will snap necks and clog city streets for hours.

"And that's the point, because it drives exactly like an LP640, right down to the paddle-shift gearbox that hates and jerks its way through the multi-point turns the wide turning circle [12 meters] demands. It's this system that is probably the low-light, particularly on a car with a €1 million price tag on it. Plus tax."

Still, at least the carbon-ceramic brake discs that were a very necessary option on the Murciélago came as standard. In any case, the rarefied price didn't act as a

disincentive to purchase; Lamborghini had an orderly line of over 20 putative buyers after just one showing of a quarter-scale model in Santa Monica, California.

For those unlucky enough to miss the opportunity to buy one of the 20 Reventóns in 2007, Lamborghini obliged two years later with something equally stunning—but rarer still. As the wraps came off the Reventón Roadster at the 2009 Frankfurt Motor Show, 12 of the 15 examples to be built had already been sold. The price tag? €1.1 million. At this rarefied level, the frigid outlook for the global economy held little relevance: this, for sure, was a cast iron investment as well as an object of singular beauty.

Powers of hyperbole temporarily deserted Lamborghini's product planners as they named the Roadster's color, which was similar to the coupe's but a couple of grades lighter, "Reventón Grey." Again, the matte metallic looked sensational in the flesh, set off neatly against glossy Y-spoked alloy wheels with matte carbon winglets that were reckoned to aid brake cooling.

The Reventón Roadster gained just 25 kilograms in the process of losing its roof, since the existing spaceframe structure was claimed to have sufficient torsional rigidity without too much additional bracing being required. As with the coupe, the bodywork was mostly composite, with the exception of the skins of the scissor doors, which were steel. Most of the Roadster's modest weight gain can be accounted for by the mechanisms behind each seat designed to rapidly deploy a pair of roll hoops if they detect that the car is in the process of turning over. The other addition was a cross-member behind the seats with a high-level brake light—a mandatory safety feature in many countries. As with the coupe—and, indeed, the Murciélago—the trailing edge of the rear deck doubled as a stability-boosting wing that moved automatically to two different angles of attack, the first at 80 miles per hour and the second at 136 miles per hour.

To (over)compensate for the additional weight, Lamborghini gifted the Roadster the most powerful derivative of the V-12 in its arsenal, the SV. Boasting 670 PS (661 brake horsepower), this gave an extra 20 brake horsepower over and above the additional 10 brake horsepower gained by the coupe. Thus, the Roadster lost nothing in theoretical performance, completing the 0–60 miles per hour dash in a claimed 3.4 seconds, while its driver got to enjoy the soundtrack of a mighty V-12 lump that was blood-curdling enough when fully enclosed in the Murciélago SV. It was spectacular at rest, too, because the Reventón Roadster's rear deck had a more extensive glazed area than the coupe's, offering walk-by spectators a tantalizing view of the merchandise.

With the Roadster's targa roof off, passers-by also got a better view of the Reventón's spectacular Alcantara-trimmed cabin. Owners would probably prefer them not to touch, which was a pity, because much of the real estate within was highly tactile: the housing for the liquid-crystal dashboard displays, for instance, was CNC-milled from aluminum billet and trimmed in carbon fiber.

As Lamborghini's brand director, Manfred Fitzgerald, said: "Many people around the world require a practical justification for buying such a car, but buyers in this league are more willing to indulge life. It's not a question here of straightforward product benefits, but of a work of art. We're selling dreams."

Reventón

Chassis	Tubular steel monocoque
Suspension	Independent double wishbones front/rear, coaxial coil springs, telescopic shock absorbers, anti-roll bars, and anti-squat bars
Brakes	Ventilated carbon-ceramic discs with ABS, ASR, and ABD
Wheelbase	2665 mm
Front/rear track	1635 mm/1695 mm
Wheels/Tires	18 in × 8.5 in, Pirelli PZero 245/35 (front); 18 in × 13 in, Pirelli PZero 335/30 (rear)
Engine	Rear longitudinal-mounted 60-degree V-12
Bore/Stroke	88 mm/89 mm
Cubic capacity	6496 cc
Compression ratio	11.0:1
Maximum power	641 bhp at 8000 rpm (Roadster 661 bhp at 8000 rpm)
Valve gear	Dual overhead camshafts, chain drive, 4 valves per cylinder, continuously variable timing
Fuel/ignition system	Lamborghini electronic fuel injection, individual coils
Lubrication	Dry sump
Gearbox	Lamborghini 6-speed e-gear robotized manual
Transmission	Four-wheel drive
Clutch	Dry single-plate
Dry weight	1665 kg (Roadster 1690 kg)
Top speed	211 mph (Roadster 205 mph)

AVENTADOR

RECALIBRATING THE

WITH FORMULA 1 RACE CAR BUILDER MCLAREN joining the supercar arena, Lamborghini had another technically advanced, competent, and ambitious competitor to face as it developed a replacement for the Murciélago. All this and a sales-throttling global recession, too. It would have been easy, therefore, to serve up a warmed-over version of the Murciélago's underpinnings in a shiny new bodyshell.

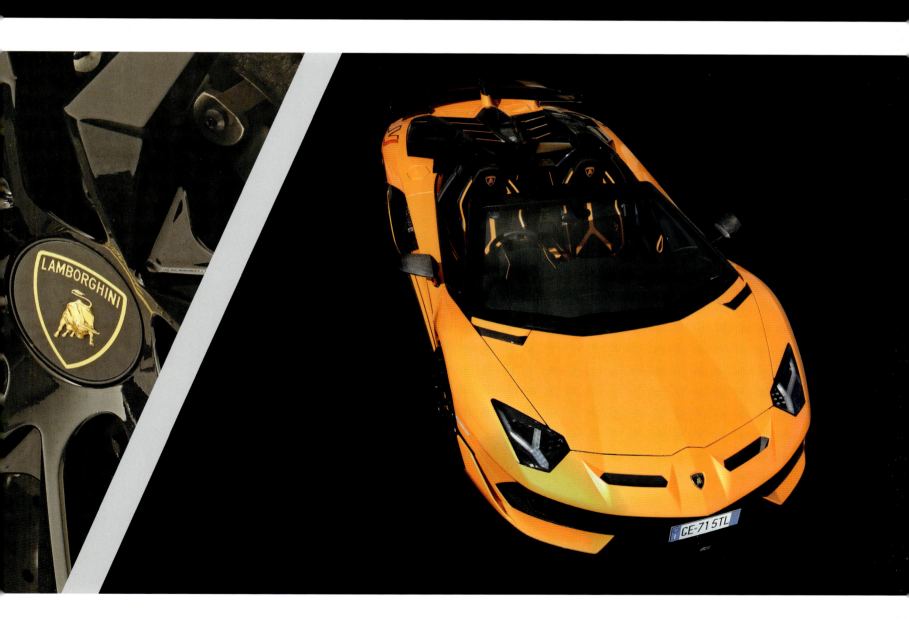

SUPERCAR FORMULA

With the Aventador, Lamborghini not only embraced monocoque chassis construction for the first time, but it also made the "tub" completely out of carbon fiber.

But Lamborghini, even under Audi's prudent ownership, has never been one to do half a job. The Aventador, which arrived in 2011, wasn't just a step forward in engineering terms—it represented, in many ways, a break from the past, though it still could not be anything other than a Lamborghini. Its pleasingly iambic nomenclature came not from a bull breeder (Miura) or a bull breed (Gallardo), but from a specific 1,118-pound fighting bovine whose career came to a bloody end at the hands of celebrated matador Emilio Munoz in the Plaza de Toros de Zaragoza in October 1993.

The chassis reversed the principles of the Murciélago, which in traditional Lamborghini style was based on a steel tube frame and largely clothed in carbon fiber panels, but for the steel roof and doors. For the Aventador, Lamborghini designed a completely new carbon fiber monocoque chassis, with aluminum subframes front and rear to carry the suspension and engine and enable an element of repairability after minor accidents. This set it on the road to a considerable weight reduction of 90 kilograms over the Murciélago, the equivalent of instructing a healthy adult passenger to take the bus instead.

Let us turn to the other part of the newer car's nomenclature: LP700-4. Dividing 691 brake horsepower (700 PS in the European methodology of power measurement, hence the name) between the four wheels compared with its predecessor's 632 brake horsepower, the Aventador gained a reasonable power bump to accompany its lower weight, but with no increase in engine displacement from 6.5 liters. The occupant of the engine bay was completely new, shorn of any link with the original Bizzarrini V-12.

Lamborghini's new-generation V-12 had a bigger bore and shorter stroke (95 millimeters × 76.4 millimeters versus 88 × 86.8), which, naturally, made it more eager to rev, although it also had greater torque than its predecessor. Although the additional horses arrived slightly higher up the rev range, peak torque came a little lower at 5500 rpm; thus, the signature Lamborghini appetite for revs was not only preserved but amplified, along with the muscular bellow, in a more accessible package.

The extrovertly crisp-edged styling of the Aventador was the work of former Alfa Romeo designer Filippo Perini, who cited fighter jets as inspiration for the car's neat integration of form and function: all the bodywork apertures serve radiators, brake ducts, or air intakes, albeit with an artistic flourish. The body flares outward at the rear in typical Lamborghini style before folding sharply back on itself in a flurry of insectoid zigzags, capped by a retracting tail spoiler that only deploys at speed. While its outline is simple, and largely composed of unbroken flowing lines, the Aventador's flamboyant V-shaped detailing recalls the stark functionality of the Northrop B-2 Spirit "stealth bomber" and Lockheed F-117 Nighthawk. Lamborghini Centro Stile, you feel, is staffed by people unfazed by the knowledge that their work must be nothing less than stunning. Acknowledged Perini:

> A designer working here has a *little problem*. He has to design something that respects the quantity and the quality of the work done by past designers, while bearing comparison with iconic cars such as the Miura, Countach, Murciélago, and Diablo. Just think of these names; our cars almost always become design icons.
>
> We are the only supercar brand that can afford to build a car with a single line connecting front and rear. This is achieved through the package itself: all the masses and mechanical components are contained within the wheelbase. Then we vary the recipe. We can add some sensuality to the line that connects the fender to the belt line in a fluid, clean way. The upper section of the car is linear; in the side view we have another important line that flows in space in a very important way—this is the "tornado line" that connects the front of the car to the tip of the spoiler.
>
> One of the departures from the Murciélago is the position of the engine radiators at the side, where the need for an air opening enabled us to create an extremely sculpted surface.
>
> While for the overall design we took inspiration from aeronautics, the rear was a big departure. The rear surface angle is the reverse of what we are used to seeing, which creates a dynamic effect.

Also new was the seven-speed ISR (Independent Shifting Rod) automated manual gearbox, which, while not offering quite the panache of the VW Group's twin-clutch DSG system, was faster than the Gallardo's e-drive—offering shift times of 50 milliseconds—and at 70 kilograms it was lighter and more compact than DSG. At launch, Lamborghini promised the transmission would convey an "emotional shifting feel" and that gear shifts would occur "virtually in parallel." In theory, while one shifting rod moves out of gear, another is engaging the next one; there are four shifting rods in all, each hydraulically actuated via a high-pressure system running at 60 bar.

As was modish at the time, the manner of the gear change was driver-selectable according to three modes: Strada, Sport, and Corsa. Strada was envisioned as an everyday use mode, with a focus on comfort, offering fully automatic shifting. Sport was a more aggressive performance mode, while the track-biased Corsa mode gave the fastest shifts. As ever with such systems, these were quickly outed as a pointless gimmick; no road tester worth their salt, and very few customers, were interested in cruising around in fully automatic mode, and Corsa was just too violent for everyday use (*Road & Track* wrote that it "bangs cogs home like a Top Fuel car leaving the line"). The launch control function would win most traffic light grands prix; the driver slams the gear home and the car springs away from a standing start with a minimum of wheel chatter at the cost of a sensation akin to being rear-ended by a 10-ton truck.

Though lighter than its forebears, the Aventador occupies a similar amount of road real estate; and while its cockpit offers more room for its occupants to flex their limbs, thanks to the more compact drivetrain, luggage capacity stretches no further than a small compartment up front and a slim pair of pockets in the leather-lined cabin. Never mind: the genuine millionaire can get by with just their wallet, buy a new wardrobe at their destination, and then leave its contents for the maid at checkout.

Still, as ever when a new supercar is launched into a chilly economic climate, the Aventador prompted some scribes to consider the philosophical implications of owning such an extravagantly impractical conveyance. Andrew Frankel wrote in *Autocar*:

> As a thing to drive, the Aventador is as safe as anyone could reasonably expect a 691bhp supercar with sub-3.0sec 0–62mph capability to be, but as a device to distract other drivers from the road ahead, its powers may be unprecedented. You might never crash yourself, but you're going to see plenty. But is this not exactly what owners seek from such a car? Is a Lamborghini Aventador, like its forefathers the Murciélago, Diablo and Countach, not an attention-seeking device first and a thoroughbred driving machine second? Maybe, but that doesn't mean its existence is not to be celebrated. Among mainstream production cars—which excludes esoteric models such as Paganis and Koenigseggs built in single or double-digit numbers—the Aventador now stands alone. Although the Aventador is laden with state-of-the-art technology, at its heart it remains a supercar of the old school, a massively wide, impossibly low machine powered by an outrageously powerful and classic normally aspirated V12—words that would have applied no less accurately to the Countach at its first public showing more than 40 years ago.

As with any supercar in development, the Aventador wore a heavy disguise during track testing at the prototype stage to thwart "scoop" photographers.

Arancio Argos joined the Lamborghini palette for the Aventador's launch and has become one of the most popular color choices for the car.

Limited to 800 examples, the track-focused Aventador SVJ Roadster is 50kg heavier than the Coupé on account of the additional chassis bracing required to compensate for the absence of a roof panel. It's just 0.1s slower in the 0-62 miles per hour benchmark, and quoted top speed is identical thanks to the presence of active aerodynamics.

Aventador LP700-4 Roadster

Chassis	Carbon fiber monocoque, aluminum front/rear frames
Suspension	Push-rod-actuated horizontal mono-tube dampers front/rear
Brakes	Carbon-ceramic with 6-piston calipers front, 4-piston calipers rear
Wheelbase	2700 mm
Front/rear track	1720 mm/1700 mm
Wheels/Tires	19 in × 9J, Pirelli PZero 255/35 ZR19 (front); 20 in × 12J, Pirelli PZero 335/30 (rear)
Engine	Rear longitudinally mounted 60-degree V-12
Bore/Stroke	95 mm/76.4 mm
Cubic capacity	6498 cc
Compression ratio	11.8/1
Maximum power	690 bhp at 8250 rpm
Valve gear	Dual overhead camshafts; electronically controlled variable valve timing
Fuel/ignition system	Lamborghini electronic fuel injection
Lubrication	Dry sump
Gearbox	Lamborghini 7-speed ISR
Transmission	Haldex IV four-wheel drive
Clutch	Dry double-plate
Dry weight	1625 kg
Top speed	217 mph

Removal of the roof does not detract from the Aventador's appearance, but the carbon fiber panels that act as a temporary hard top eat up luggage space when stowed.

AVENTADOR ROADSTER

OPPOSITE: The Aventador SVJ Roadster's twin carbon fiber roof panels weigh just 6kg each – but, if you want to take them with you when you're driving with the roof off, they take up all the available space in the luggage compartment…

If in the unlikely event that the Aventador did not provide enough theater, Lamborghini resolved that issue by launching a roofless model in 2013, along with a new color, Azzuro Thetis, a timeless pale blue hue that evoked Mediterranean idyll. As a piece of engineering, the Roadster was remarkable; yes, the removal of the roof necessitated additional structural bracing, and therefore weight (to the tune of 50 kilograms), but in pure performance terms that amounted to . . . not very much. It would be persnickety indeed to declaim the Roadster as a lemon because its benchmark 0.62-miles per hour time was 0.1 seconds slower than its roofed sibling's. In any case the top speed, should you find a road long, straight, and unpoliced enough, was identical at 217 miles per hour

Better still, design chief Filippo Perini had actioned the drop top with exquisite care, resulting in a car that to some eyes was even more beautiful—if that were possible—than the coupe. Its temporary hard top came in the form of two six-kilogram carbon fiber panels, both delightfully crafted, which could be removed in moments and stowed in the luggage compartment under the hood.

And there, as Shakespeare put it, lies the rub. With the roof off and the panels occupying the luggage compartment, the adventurous Aventador owner would have to sally forth equipped with not much more than his or her cellphone and a toothbrush. It would be churlish to point out the impracticality of this arrangement, but, still, someone had to do it.

"So," one American journalist asked Lamborghini CEO Stephan Winkelmann during a Q&A at the car's launch in Miami, "what do we do with our luggage? Send it by FedEx?"

The urbane and well-educated Winkelmann batted the question out of the park without missing a beat: "You travel to your destination with the roof up, then, when you've checked in to your hotel, and your bags are out of the car, you can have some fun with the roof off."

The launch of the Roadster coincided with the rollout of new gear shift software on both models that was intended to make ratio changes more civilized, but the transmission still left many test drivers discombobulated.

"Fast up-shifts are still akin to being kicked in the head," complained Jason Barlow in *Top Gear*. "Maybe Lamborghinis are meant to be borderline thuggish, but the transmission remains deeply flawed. In full auto mode around town, it's arguably even worse, a lurching throwback to the earliest days of semi-autos, when dinosaurs still roamed the land. Dual-shift gearboxes might be heavy and difficult to package, but once you've tried a good one there's no going back."

Cro-Magnon transmission apart, there was no doubt that the Aventador—in both coupe and Roadster forms—still offered a driving experience like no other. "As absurd as it sounds for a £294,665 [$441,000] car, the Aventador Roadster is good value," concluded Nick Trott, editor of the UK-based performance car bible *Evo*. "There is no other new rival (on price) that can get close to delivering the wildly acute supercar experience. There are greater driving thrills to be had from the Ferrari 458, and a McLaren 12C feels every bit as quick, but to enjoy a more visceral supercar you need to spend another £500,000 [$829,000] on a Pagani Huayra. Saying that, the Pagani's (AMG-made) engine is nowhere near as charismatic as the Lamborghini's."

True. This was a car about sight and sound. Just don't expect to converse with your passenger over 75 miles per hour.

Arriving in 2015, the lighter, faster, Aventador SV featured a larger rear wing, magnetic suspension, carbon-ceramic brakes and a new electronic steering system to deliver a more track-like feel.

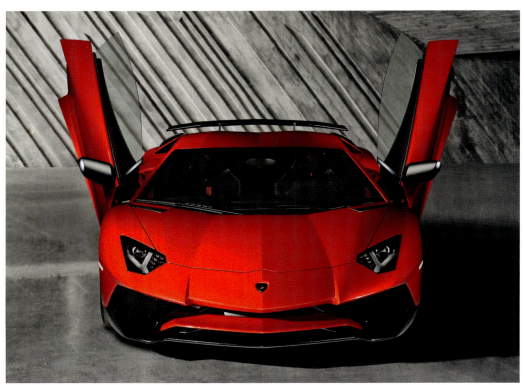

Perhaps as a concession to a slightly older demographic—on launch, prices started at $392,000, and bankers' bonuses were under scrutiny at the time—entry and egress is easier and more elegant, owing to the lower sills and friendlier door apertures, and the seats are softer. The controls are laid out with an element of logic and can be reached without leaving the driver's seat. The all-digital Gran Turismo–style instrument panel proved to be an acquired taste for many owners, but it put very few people off; the first year's production run was sold out even before the first customers took delivery in the summer of 2011, and the 2,000th Aventador left the production line two years later. Lamborghini had built only 2,042 Countachs in the course of its 16-year life.

For those with a mind to drive, rather than pose, the Aventador offered a challenging but much more accessible experience than its predecessors, genuinely blurring the dividing line between supercar and hypercar. The Haldex IV all-wheel-drive system gave superb traction, delivering all 691 brake horsepower to the road with barely a chirrup of protest from the enormous tires. Considering its imposing physicality and fairly substantial weight, it changed direction quickly and offered incredible lateral grip.

Aventador LP700-4

Chassis	Carbon fiber monocoque, aluminum front/rear frames
Suspension	Pushrod-actuated horizontal mono-tube dampers front/rear
Brakes	Carbon-ceramic with 6-piston calipers front, 4-piston calipers rear
Wheelbase	2700 mm
Front/rear track	1720 mm/1700 mm
Wheels/Tires	19 in × 9J, Pirelli PZero 255/35 ZR19 (front); 20 in × 12J, Pirelli PZero 335/30 (rear)
Engine	Rear longitudinally mounted 60-degree V-12
Bore/Stroke	95 mm/76.4 mm
Cubic capacity	6498 cc
Compression ratio	11.8:1
Maximum power	690 bhp at 8250 rpm
Valve gear	Dual overhead camshafts; electronically controlled variable valve timing
Fuel/ignition system	Lamborghini electronic fuel injection
Lubrication	Dry sump
Gearbox	Lamborghini 7-speed ISR
Transmission	Haldex IV four-wheel drive
Clutch	Dry double-plate
Dry weight	1575 kg
Top speed	217 mph

But this came with a small caveat: the limits were so high, and the car so wide, that you could only sensibly explore the fringes of its capabilities on track—as, of course, with so many Lamborghini supercars past.

"With enough space," wrote Chris Chilton in *Road & Track*, "the Aventador can be coaxed into a slide, but you'd be coaxed into a rear-fastening cardigan if you tried it on the road. Choose neat, choose to live. . . . You tread the line between grip and slip in the Lamborghini as if you're hiking across the demilitarized zone between North and South Korea."

This reality did not dissuade Lamborghini from expanding the Aventador's performance envelope. The LP 720-4 50th Anniversario limited-edition model (100 coupes, 100 roadsters), which marked the company's 50th year in business, featured a modest power hike to 710 brake horsepower, complemented by aerodynamic revisions around the nose and engine cover. It sold so quickly that Lamborghini could not resist returning to the trough many times during the Aventador's life, contriving a growing array of one-offs and limited-run specials.

As rivals began to offer more track-focused variants of their supercars, Lamborghini cleaved to trends with the LP750-4 Superveloce. Tweaked aerodynamics—including a huge fixed rear wing—delivered a claimed 180 percent downforce gain over

The Aventador S Coupé (following page) and Roadster received a light facelift in 2017 along with a dynamic boost: engine power rose to 730bhp, while a four-wheel steering system and revised suspension made it slightly less brutal and uncompromising to drive.

AVENTADOR J

How much great art has been conjured by whim alone? The eye-popping Aventador J, which stopped the 2012 Geneva Motor Show in its tracks, was produced in just a month and a half after Lamborghini CEO Stephan Winkelmann decided the manufacturer needed "something special" for the show. Design boss Filippo Perini gladly hastened to his drawing board.

"It was January 14 that Mr. Winkelmann asked us to do something for Geneva," said Perini. "A blank sheet. Do what you want. I drew up this car in a weekend. . . ."

Chassis, engine, transmission, and dashboard apart, the Aventador J shared just the hood, rear fenders, and headlights with the donor car. Every other exterior panel was new, from the Le Mans Prototype-style front wing to the twin humps behind the seats that flanked a Y-shaped carbon fiber crossbrace. The pylon-mounted rear-view mirror recalled the eccentric Eiffeland Formula 1 car of the 1970s, and the seats were similarly race-bred, formed from composite materials and a patented carbon fiber fabric.

The *J* was an explicit reference to the Miura Jota, Lamborghini's last extreme one-off car. And, needless to say, the one-off car—which was homologated for road use—had found a buyer even before it was revealed at Geneva. For $2.8 million, one of Lamborghini's best customers had laid their hands on a remarkable piece of automotive art.

the standard Aventador. More extensive use of carbon fiber emphasized its racier ambitions, but the changes were more than cosmetic. Magnetic suspension, a new electronic steering system, and carbon-ceramic brakes delivered a more track-like experience even though the old-fashioned gearbox remained a bugbear. For those who liked to lap with the wind in their hair, a roadster version followed.

Aventador sales had far exceeded the original ambition of 4,000 units when it received a midlife refresh in 2017. The new Aventador S LP740-4 gained a four-wheel steering system, an active rear wing, and reengineered suspension, all necessary to marshal the V-12's additional grunt (up to 730 brake horsepower). Lamborghini claimed the new aerodynamic arrangement boosted downforce by 130 percent. Marketing hyperbole aside, perhaps the most pleasing development was a user-programmable fourth mode in the dynamic drive system, which enabled the driver to cherry-pick the best aspects of the other three.

L539: THE ALL-NEW V-12

It was the kind of open brief engineers crave. In closing the door on five generations of the original Bizzarrini V-12, a beast whose character is enshrined in the company's very DNA, Lamborghini gave its R&D team, led by chief engineer Maurizio Reggiani, just two absolute musts: the new engine, codenamed L539, had to be a V-12, and those cylinders had to be banked at 60 degrees. This at a time when key rivals such as Ferrari were downsizing and adding turbos, if not going the whole hybrid hog.

Thus, while the L539 also turned out at 6.5 liters, the internals were treated to some fresh thinking with an eye on efficiency as well as outright power. Wider bores (up to 95 millimeters from 88) and shorter stroke (down to 76.4 millimeters from 89) account for reduced frictional losses as well as liberating more power (691 brake horsepower, up from 632) at slightly higher revs (8250 rpm). Torque rose to 509 pounds-feet at 5500 rpm from 486 pounds-feet at 6000 rpm.

Extensive use of aluminum-silicon alloy in the block and cylinder heads contributed to a lower weight of 235 kilograms—the old unit tipped the scales at 253 kilograms—even though the new V-12 had more complicated plumbing, with eight scavenging pumps to reduce pressure and switchable water circuits to expedite warm-up to optimum temperature.

Some detail elements of the engine and transmission spec were questioned at launch: direct fuel injection proved too challenging to perfect in the project's timeframe, though it hasn't been ruled out for the future. And, while the seven-speed, single-clutch ISR (Independent Shifting Rod) automated manual gearbox was lighter than the twin-clutch DSG arrangement popular elsewhere in the VW Group range, it lacked some of that transmission's sweetness . . . plus there was no manual option, which cut against some European tastes. Still, it was more compact than the outgoing transmission.

And, 50 years down the line, Bizzarrini finally got his way: the new engine was dry-sumped, making it more vertically compact, with all the benefits that brings to a car's center of gravity. He would, you feel, have approved.

Mitja Borkert, head of Lamborghini styling since 2016, prefers to work in sketches on paper before heading to the computer. "With just a few elegant and accurate lines, it is possible to create a new Lamborghini," he says.

Aventador S LP740-4

Chassis	Carbon fiber monocoque, aluminum front/rear frames
Suspension	Pushrod-actuated horizontal mono-tube dampers front/rear
Brakes	Carbon-ceramic with 6-piston calipers front, 4-piston calipers rear
Wheelbase	2700 mm
Front/rear track	1720 mm/1700 mm
Wheels/Tires	20 in × 9J, Pirelli PZero 255/30 ZR20 (front); 21 in × 13J, Pirelli PZero 355/25 ZR21 (rear)
Engine	Rear longitudinally mounted 60-degree V-12
Bore/Stroke	95 mm/76.4 mm
Cubic capacity	6498 cc
Compression ratio	11.8:1
Maximum power	740 bhp at 8400 rpm
Valve gear	Dual overhead camshafts; electronically controlled variable valve timing
Fuel/ignition system	Lamborghini multi-point electronic fuel injection
Lubrication	Dry sump
Gearbox	Lamborghini 7-speed ISR
Transmission	Haldex IV four-wheel drive
Clutch	Dry double-plate
Dry weight	1575 kg
Top speed	217 mph

New chief designer Mitja Borkert reworked the exterior sympathetically, incorporating a striking homage to the Countach in the flow of the lines around the rear wings and air intakes. New winglets beneath the front bumper evoked a snake's fangs. But the primary difference lay in the driving experience; Lamborghini had dialed back the behavior of the four-wheel-drive system to give a more rear-drive feel. At launch, Lamborghini provided an old model for journalists to evaluate alongside the new one at the Circuit Ricardo Tormo in Valencia, Spain.

"The difference isn't subtle," wrote Ben Barry in *Car* magazine. "Where the old car feels very nose-led and slightly stubborn, its steering lethargic where you need flighty flicks left-to-right, the S dances through the slalom with a balance that feels much more in line with your hips, and steering that feels light years faster."

Essentially the Aventador S demonstrated an important triumph for Lamborghini: throwing electronics at its chassis genuinely could enable it to offer a hulking great V-12 engine with very few of the downsides. In 2018, Lamborghini launched a track-focused variant of the second-generation Aventador, the LP770-40 Superveloce Jota (SVJ). Like the SV special edition of the original model, it offered more power (760 brake horsepower), aggressive lightweighting through carbon fiber and other exotic materials, and augmented aerodynamics. Active aero devices in the front and rear enabled the car to juggle drag versus downforce, while vortex generators and a huge rear diffuser made the underbody work to achieve a claimed 40 percent downforce gain over the original Aventador SV.

Despite increasing competition from rivals, Lamborghini's flagship model has thrived beyond all expectations. Over 10,000 Aventadors were built before the model was phased out, more than double an original target, which some felt overly ambitious at the time.

TAKE IT TO THE TRACK

If the Aventador SVJ isn't racily individual enough for you, just call Lamborghini's Squadra Corse racing division—provided your pockets are deep enough.

In November 2018, it showed an exclusive one-off variant of the SVJ, the SC18 Alston, built on behalf of an unnamed customer. Boasting bespoke aerodynamic furniture inspired by the racing variants of the Huracán, wheels closely related to those on the Veneno, and a rear-end visual treatment similar to that of the limited-edition Centenario, it was indubitably distinctive. The cost, like its performance figures, was never revealed.

In 2020, Lamborghini revealed another bespoke one-off, the SC20. Mitja Borkert revealed that his brief from the customer for the open-top car was simple: "Just make it look cool." As with the SC18 Alston, the donor architecture is the Aventador SVJ, while much of the furniture is bespoke, including 3D-printed air vents.

"You come to Lamborghini," said Borkert, "you get the latest configuration of the V-12, and then you get automotive haute couture design on top."

SESTO ELEMENTO

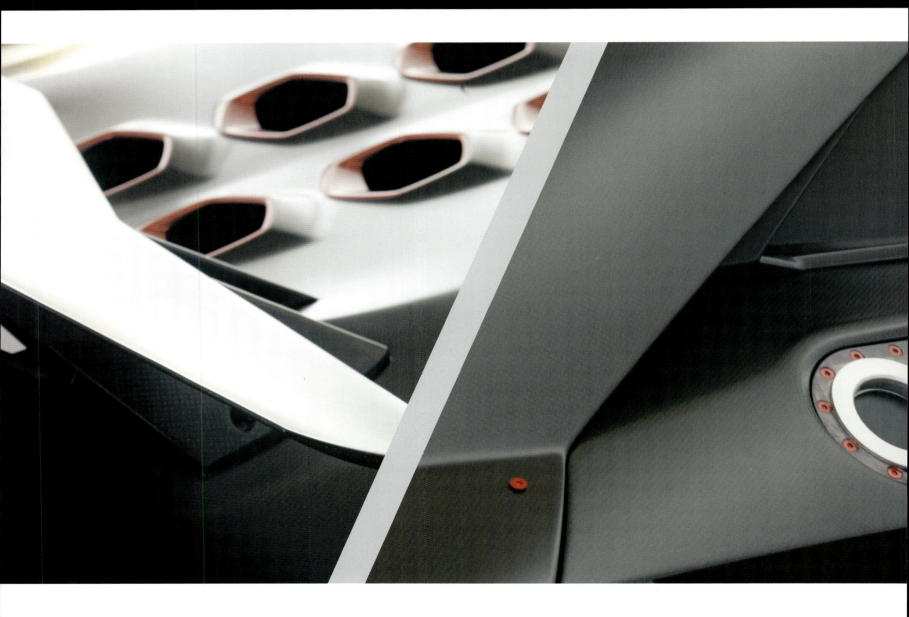

ALL THE POWER

THE SESTO ELEMENTO, unveiled to the public at the 2010 Paris Motor Show, provided yet more evidence of Lamborghini's ability to turn a whim into an object of electrifying lust. What began life as a concept car—or, in Audi-era Lamborghini parlance, "a unique technology demonstrator"—swiftly persuaded enough of the company's wealthiest customers to vote with their wallets. At Frankfurt the following year, Lamborghini announced that a limited production run would become available in 2013, priced over $2 million; they were all sold before the first (of 20) was completed.

NONE OF THE WEIGHT

Its name riffs on the periodic table of the elements, the sixth of which is carbon. Extensive use of carbon fiber all through the car's construction enabled Lamborghini to make it "extremely lightweight," although when you're talking about a car occupying this much real estate, and with a V-10 engine and all-wheel drive, these things are relative: it still tipped the scales at 2,202 pounds, just under 1,000 kilograms. Still, that's under two-thirds the weight of a Chevrolet Corvette C7 (3,298 pounds), and much lighter than the Gallardo LP 570-4 Superleggera (2,954 pounds) that donated the drivetrain. When you consider that the standard Gallardo, which is in the same dimensional ballpark as the Sesto Elemento, weighed 3,307 pounds, you'll appreciate how rigorous the paring-down process must have been.

This car represented a strategic shift to embrace ongoing changes in the automotive world, namely the need to increase efficiency—or to be seen to be doing so. It's a troubling proposition for any supercar manufacturer, but especially one whose brand is predicated upon brutal, muscular performance. Thus, rather than downsizing its engines, Lamborghini targeted extreme weight loss.

EGOISTA

If the Veneno and its Roadster variant were mere "celebrations" of Lamborghini's 50th anniversary, the Egoista was Lamborghini's birthday present to itself—or, more accurately, a token of esteem from the parent group for the brand's rebirth and runaway success. Shown to the public—well, a select gathering of VIPs—for the first time at the end of a massive 350-vehicle grand tour of Italy, the sole Egoista was driven by company president and CEO Stephan Winkelmann onto a stage that had been designed to mimic a landing strip.

Based on Gallardo underpinnings, the most extreme Lamborghini show car ever was actually designed by VW stylists under the eye of Group Head of Design Walter de Silva. The sharply creased exterior, with a single-seat cockpit influenced by the Apache helicopter and the hunched fenders shaped to suggest a bull with its horns down, ready to charge, was the work of Alessandro Dambrosio.

"The bull is driving towards the front wheels," claimed the Lamborghini press materials, "conferring a futuristic dynamism and lines which are already, in themselves, highly aggressive."

De Silva explained the rationale behind the single seat: "This is a car made for one person only, to allow them to have fun and express their personality to the maximum. It is designed purely for hyper-sophisticated people who want only the most extreme and special things in the world. It represents hedonism taken to the extreme; it is a car without compromises, in a word: egoista [selfish]."

The cockpit was a confection of aluminum and carbon fiber and actually removable, in the same way that the cockpit of an Apache helicopter doubles as a survival cell and can be ejected when the aircraft is in trouble. Interior designer Stefan Sielaff mingled cues from fighter aircraft with race cars, specifying a futuristic heads-up display, a four-point harness, and a steering wheel that has to be removed in order for the driver to effect entry and egress. There was even a specified method of getting in and out, complete with no-walk zones indicated on the bodywork, as on airplane wings.

No modern Lamborghini is complete without stealth fighter overtones, and the Egoista combined UFO-for-the-road lighting effects—on first glance it doesn't have headlights as such, but aircraft-style LED clearance lights—with bodywork made from composites finished in an anti-radar material, plus a pair of moveable flaps on the rear deck. The twin xenon headlights are concealed in the void between the nose cone and the fender pontoons.

The 592-brake-horsepower Gallardo-derived V-10 itself was left on display to aid cooling, add a note of aggression, and to encourage spectators to gawp.

"If Lamborghinis are cars for the few, this one goes further," summarized the press materials. "It is a car for itself, a gift from Lamborghini to Lamborghini, resplendent in its solitude. The Egoista is pure emotion, Never Never Land, which no one can ever possess, and which will always remain a dream, for everyone."

Such extreme whimsy was not for everyone, and the Egoista certainly polarized the Internet commentariat, but seen in the metal (and carbon fiber) it is an extraordinary piece of work. It is now permanently on display in the Lamborghini Museum, where you can judge for yourself.

Lamborghini President and CEO Stephan Winkelmann was unequivocal: "The Sesto Elemento shows how the future of the super sports car can look—extreme lightweight engineering, combined with extreme performance, results in extreme driving fun. We put all of our technological competence into one stunning form to create the Sesto Elemento. It is our abilities in carbon fiber technology that have facilitated such a forward-thinking concept, and we of course also benefit from the undisputed lightweight expertise of Audi. Systematic lightweight engineering is crucial for future super sports cars: for the most dynamic performance, as well as for low emissions. We will apply this technological advantage right across our model range. Every future Lamborghini will be touched by the spirit of the Sesto Elemento."

Beyond the glitter of marketing hyperbole, how did Lamborghini do it? The secret lies in the detailing, which is exquisite and imaginative. Naturally the monocoque is carbon fiber, as per the Aventador (which was in the late stages of development when the Sesto Elemento was unveiled, and launched in 2011); the seat moldings also form part of the "tub," dressed with ultra-thin padding. To adjust the driving position, the occupant has to move the pedals and steering column relative to the fixed seat.

The front subframe, crash structures, and exterior panels are formed in carbon fiber-reinforced polymer, which Lamborghini claimed as a first, saying, "The super sports car brand from Sant'Agata Bolognese is the only vehicle manufacturer in the world to have mastered the complete CFRP process across a range of technologies, from 3D design through simulation, validation, production, and testing—all in a state-of-the-art industrial process that stands for the very highest quality standards."

The rear subframe, incorporating the engine mounts and rear suspension contacts, is aluminum, while the exterior construction gives a salutary nod toward the Miura. The bodyshell is actually two elaborate single-piece moldings (the roof is part of the monocoque) front and rear, which Lamborghini called "cofango covers" with the aerodynamic components bonded in. The doors are each made of just two separate moldings, bonded together, while the exhaust tailpipes are a glass-ceramic matrix composite called Pyrosic. Most of the suspension components are carbon fiber.

Lamborghini's expertise in composites is not just marketing bluster; the company holds a number of patents and has partnered with a number of others, including Boeing during development of the 787 Dreamliner, to create new molding technologies. In 2007 it founded the Automobili Lamborghini Advanced Composite Structures Laboratory at the University of Washington in Seattle, partly funded by Boeing and the Federal Aviation Administration.

The Sesto Elemento was the first car to demonstrate what Lamborghini calls Forged Composite technology, which was developed in collaboration with Callaway, a golfing equipment manufacturer. Forged Composite is an incredibly dense carbon fiber-epoxy molding material, with around 500,000 intertwined turbostratic (a crystalline structure in which the basal planes are out of alignment) fibers per square inch. This can be hot-pressed into a mold, rather than the traditional composite technique of layering woven sheets of carbon fiber into a mold with resin, sealing it in a vacuum, and then "curing" it under pressure in an autoclave. The upshot: more complex shapes, and the material is just as strong in every direction.

"The introduction of the Forged Composite technology allowed Lamborghini to realize the monocoque and the suspension arms of the Sesto Elemento with groundbreaking quality and costs levels," said the company's head of R&D, Maurizio Reggiani. "Our next challenge is to make this technology a standard for low-volume productions."

Speed of production remains a challenge for car manufacturers working with composites in the traditional way. McLaren's F1 was the first supercar to feature a carbon fiber monocoque, but just that part of the car required 3,500 man hours to complete. Modern techniques have reduced that amount, but it remains an expense that's ultimately passed on to the customer; hence the fact that carbon fiber construction remains the province of automotive exotica.

Lamborghini also holds a number of patents for its "RTM Lambo" production process, with RTM standing for Resin Transfer Molding. This gives a number of advantages over the traditional carbon fiber lay-up process; it can be cured without using an autoclave, so the molds can be lighter, and it can be more highly automated, so it's

quicker. The disadvantage is that the cosmetic appearance is less optimal, so for exterior panels the conventional method is still preferred, because it can be left unpainted to show off the woven finish that customers associate with carbon fiber. On the Sesto Elemento, the body panels have a patented final coat in matte, with a layer of fine red crystals that give a shimmering red effect.

The incredible power-to-weight ratio of the Sesto Elemento gave it extraordinary performance, though the race car-style suspension made it suitable for track use only, and it is not street legal. When a privileged few road testers had the opportunity to sample the demonstrator, they confirmed what everyone expected: the Sesto Elemento makes a glorious noise, but it isn't a car to be trifled with, hitting the 0–62 miles per hour benchmark in a claimed 2.5 seconds. The anonymous racing driver known as "The Stig" on the BBC's *Top Gear* TV show managed to spin it, damaging the undertray, during a recording session at Dunsfold, the former airfield in southern England that now doubles as a test track as well as a location for movies such as *Casino Royale* and *World War Z*.

Appropriately, Sesto Elemento values are now spiraling like the budget of a Hollywood blockbuster: the highest reported price paid for one is $2.9 million.

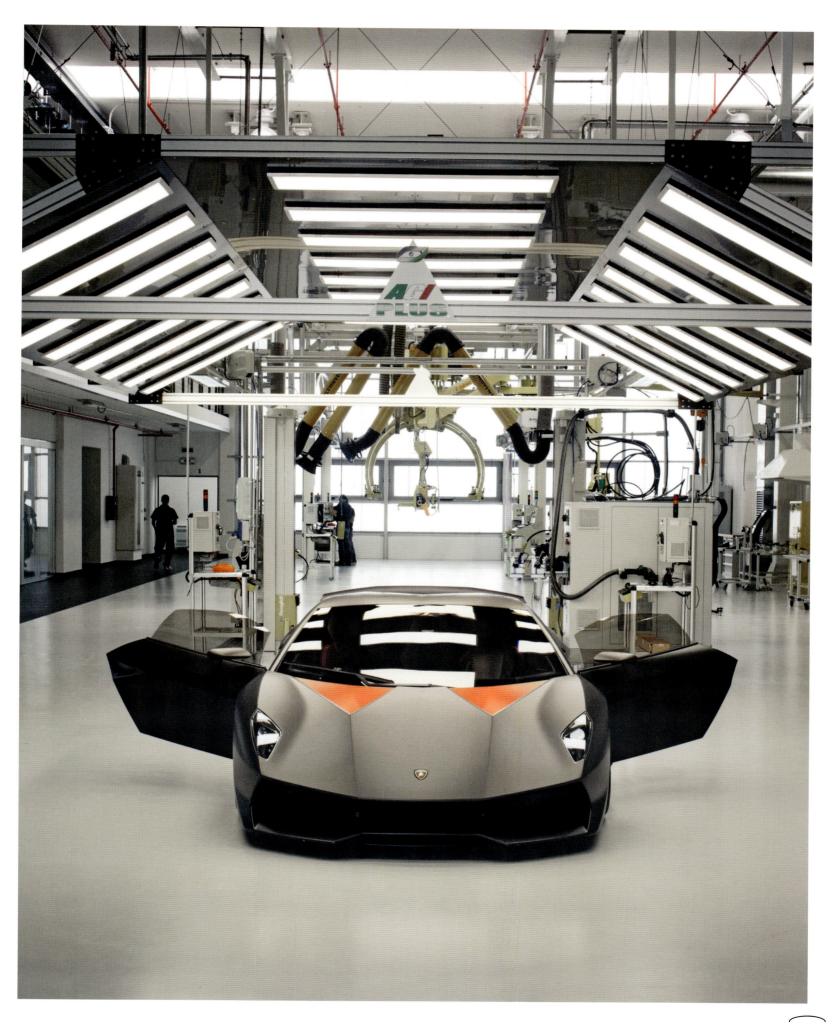

VENENO

After proving it could do boutique supercars with the Reventón, Lamborghini returned to the idea with a vengeance as part of the company's 50th anniversary celebrations. The Veneno, shown to the public at the 2013 Geneva show, was startlingly outré—like a racing version of the Aventador designed for a championship yet to be invented.

Just as the Reventón was in essence a re-skinned Murciélago, the Veneno took the composite monocoque, 6.5-liter V-12 four-wheel-drive drivetrain, and pushrod suspension of the Aventador and added an even more eye-catching shell.

Finished in modish black, the wheels (20-inch front, 21-inch rear) were sculpted to act as turbines, boosting the flow of air to the carbon-ceramic brake discs. And as a final performance touch, Lamborghini uprated the engine to deliver 750 PS (739 brake horsepower). Little wonder the company christened the car Veneno, after the bull that fatally gored toreador Jose Sanchez Rodriguez in the Sanlucar de Barrameda in 1914.

Just three examples of the Veneno were built, with a sticker price of €3 million each.

Just over a year later, Lamborghini pulled the wraps off a drop-top version of the Veneno—but, having decided that doing so at a motor show was just so *done*, it found a more outlandish platform: on the deck of an Italian aircraft carrier moored just off the coast of Abu Dhabi. The choice of that oil-rich Emirate was no coincidence; this part of the world is a hotspot for high-net-worth individuals looking to diversify their wealth away from oil, and Abu Dhabi is home to the world's first Ferrari theme park (Mubadala, an Abu Dhabi government investment fund, briefly owned a 5 percent stake in Ferrari).

Perhaps the neatest marketing trick was to make the car slightly less exclusive than the coupe—nine were built, as opposed to three—and more expensive, at €3.3 million plus local taxes.

ESSENZA SCV12

In 2021, Lamborghini took the lightweighting process to even greater extremes with the limited-edition Essenza SCV12, an Aventador-based track-only hypercar. Developed by Squadra Corse, Lamborghini's racing arm, the Essenza SCV12 is the ultimate track-day special—and, though not homologated for racing (just forty were built), the car's carbon-fiber roll cage is the first of its kind in production and meets the FIA's strict type approval standards for the Hypercar racing class.

It also acted as a farewell for the naturally aspirated V-12 in its present form. And what a stupendously noisy one: Shorn of normal road car limitations such as emissions paraphernalia, the 6.5-liter V-12 produced 818 brake horsepower, 59 brake horsepower more than the equivalent in the Aventador SVJ. Part of that boost is accounted for by a motorcycle-style ram air intake system, described by Lamborghini as "aerodynamic supercharging." Dropping the all-wheel-drive transmission in favor of a six-speed RWD setup from Xtrac cut weight, as did magnesium wheels (wrapped in bespoke Pirelli slick tires). The interior was also stripped back and featured a race-style steering wheel. In all, the Essenza SCV12 was 300 pounds (136 kilograms) lighter than the Aventador SVJ.

Though no race series (yet) exists to serve it, the Essenza SCV12 represents a new revenue stream for Lamborghini, one already adopted by rivals Ferrari and McLaren: arrive-and-drive experiences. The $2.5-million car comes with a two-year support package, which includes coaching from experienced race drivers at Lambo-organized events, plus storage, maintenance, and transport of the vehicle.

Sesto Elemento

Chassis	Carbon fiber monocoque, aluminum rear frame
Suspension	N/A
Brakes	N/A
Wheelbase	N/A
Front/rear track	N/A
Wheels/Tires	N/A
Engine	Rear longitudinally mounted 90-degree V-10
Bore/Stroke	84.5 mm/92.8 mm
Cubic capacity	5204 cc
Compression ratio	12.5:1
Maximum power	570 bhp at 8000 rpm
Valve gear	Dual overhead camshafts; electronically controlled variable valve timing
Fuel/ignition system	Bosch MED 9
Lubrication	Dry sump
Gearbox	Lamborghini 6-speed e-Gear
Transmission	Permanent four-wheel drive
Dry weight	999 kg
Top speed	N/A

HURACÁN

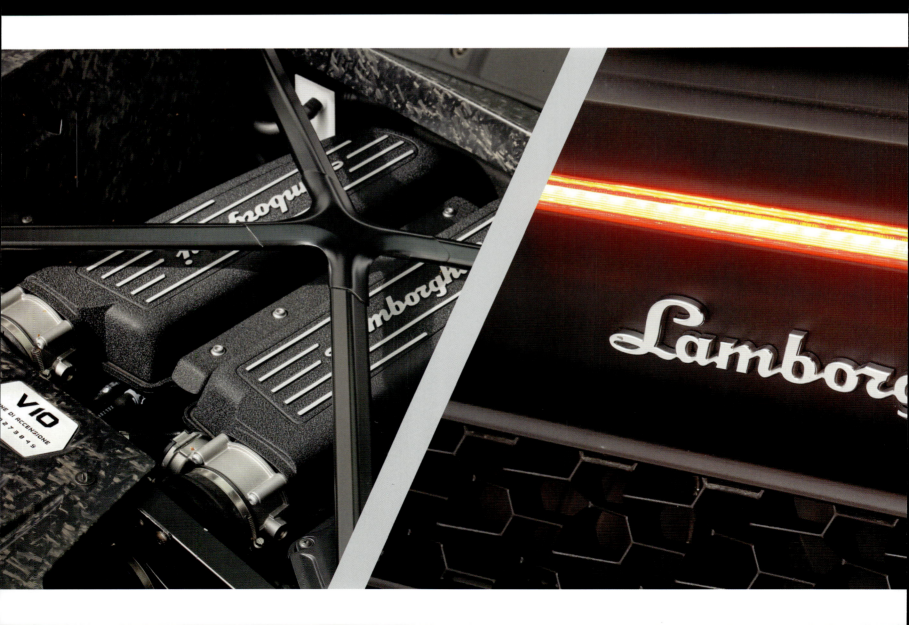

HOW DO YOU REPLACE THE MOST SUCCESSFUL LAMBORGHINI SUPERCAR OF ALL TIME? The fatuous answer is to say "very carefully." A more nuanced response, and one closer to the truth, is to suggest that you don't replace it at all; you have to offer something completely different, with its own identity, that can fill the now-vacant slot in the range for a more affordable Lamborghini. Not a replacement, but a successor.

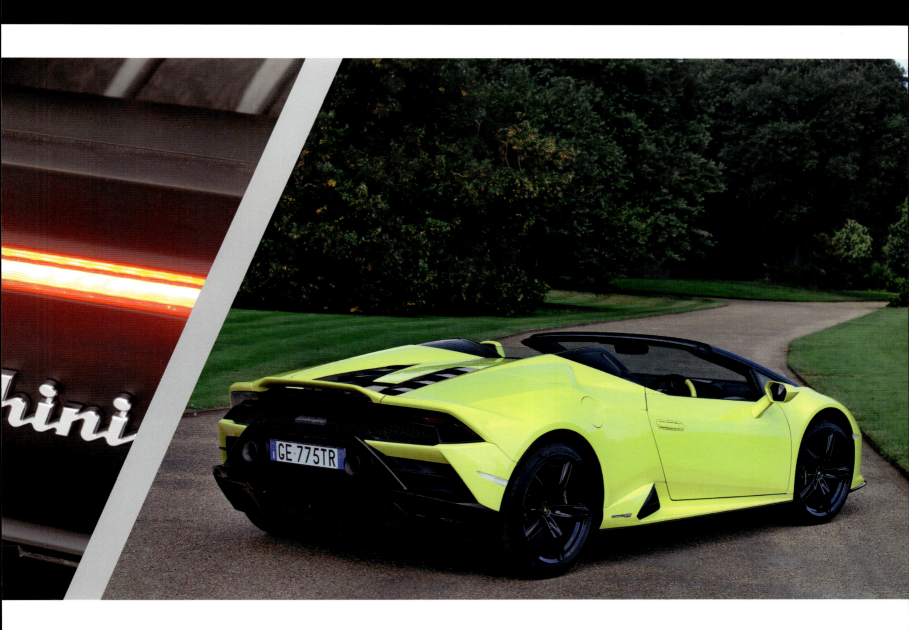

THE FUTURE IS NOW

Seven-speed dual-clutch transmission is new to Lamborghini; the Huracán is not available with a manual gearbox.

Filippo Perini sketched the first outlines of what would become the Huracán in 2009, at which point it was simply referred to by its internal code name of LB724. These early drawings followed the stealth aircraft theme he was successfully mashing up with insectoid shapes to great effect in the Reventón, while genuinely exploring the boundaries of conventional proportions. Around the flanks and at the rear it bulged like the carapace of an exotic beetle liberated from a Victorian explorer's trophy case. Later sketches reverted to Gallardo themes, straighter-edged and with large, angular hexagonal air intakes at the front. An idea took root and Perini would incorporate many hexagonal themes in the finished design.

But there was more than just the look of the car at stake. During the Gallardo's life cycle, Ferrari had refreshed its offering at that price point twice, and McLaren had launched the 12C. Ferrari's 458 Italia was a remarkably competent and characterful machine that shamelessly riffed on the company's F1 connections—even down to the manettino dials on the steering wheel—while shielding ham-fisted drivers from their own stupidity with a number of delightfully light-touch stability control systems. Its 4.5-liter direct injection V-8 engine was a match for the Gallardo's V-10, producing 562 brake horsepower in standard form, and its adaptive magnetorheological dampers helped deliver impeccable road and track manners. McLaren's carbon-tub 12C was clearly benchmarked almost slavishly to the 458 Italia, to the extent that the two were largely indistinguishable save for the character of the McLaren's smaller 3.8-liter V-8, blown with twin turbos to 592 brake horsepower.

These rivals clearly informed the development process, and it was almost a tacit admission when Lamborghini CEO Stephan Winkelmann would later say, "With the

Huracán, we wanted a car to be built with balance. The challenge for the engineers was to have a high-performance car that is easy to drive and giving you the feeling that you are a better driver than you are."

LB724 would have to be profitable as well as competitive, and this necessarily involved incorporating some Audi technical DNA while undertaking what Lambo Research & Development boss Maurizio Reggiani described as a "historical debug of the Gallardo." The spaceframe chassis—not all-aluminum like Ferrari, nor all-composite like McLaren, but a combination of the two—would be part of a shared-platform strategy, and be designed under the watchful eye of Audi R&D chief and platform-sharing champion Dr. Ulrich Hackenberg. As part of Audi's MSS (Modular Sportscar System) platform, which would also underpin the next-generation Audi R8 and other cars in the Volkswagen Group, the Huracán's chassis combined traditional aluminum spaceframe elements with composite panels made using Lamborghini's patented resin-transfer process. The carbon fiber components reinforced the floor, sills, transmission tunnel, bulkhead, and B-pillar, and were bonded to the main structure with stainless steel fasteners (sealed to prevent galvanic corrosion) in strategic areas. This would reduce weight by 10 percent (giving the complete car a dry weight of 1,422 kilograms) while improving torsional stiffness by a claimed 50 percent.

The engine and four-wheel-drive transmission would occupy its traditional *longitudinale posteriore* location but differ in several details, not least in the departure of the Gallardo's much-derided six-speed robotized manual gearbox in favor of an Oerlikon Graziano dual-clutch setup. Badged Lamborghini Doppia Frizione in this application, the seven-speed was adjustable, like its predecessor, into different shift modes to reflect how purposeful the driver wanted to be. At this level of performance, packaging a dual-clutch system is tricky, but Lamborghini was able to mount the Huracán's gearbox lower than the Gallardo's and with a slightly smaller clutch diameter (200 millimeters as opposed to 215).

To tackle the challenge of wrestling more power from the Gallardo V-10 while remaining within emissions regulations, Lamborghini raised the compression ratio to 12.7:1 and conjured an elaborate fueling system that combined both direct and indirect injection technology. The Iniezione Diretta Stratificata common-rail direct injection system activated at various points of the rev spectrum to improve peak power and efficiency, while an indirect multi-port injection (MPI), romantically described by Maurizio Reggiani as "the master of ceremonies," presided over startup and the majority of the rev range. This was an innately costly solution, because direct injection demands highly resilient injectors (since they are mounted in the combustion chamber) and a sophisticated, high-pressure pumping mechanism; and the mapping software required to harmonize two separate injection systems is an act in itself. But it would be worth it to combine the strengths and eliminate the weaknesses of the different injection methods; direct injection's more precise metering gives better economy, and the denser charge more power, but the different fuel-air mixture characteristics encourage carbon particulates to form. To run direct injection alone would mean the

The rear bodywork is protected from accidental damage while the V-10 and its transmission are installed within the chassis.

engine wouldn't pass the stringent Euro 6 emissions test without a particulate filter at the very least, which would have been counterproductive. In production trim, the peak power output was measured as 602 brake horsepower at 8250 rpm.

Like the transmission, the engine management was adjustable from the cockpit via a system Lamborghini called ANIMA—both the Italian word for "soul" and a slightly labored acronym (standing for Adaptive Network Intelligent Management). Its three modes—Strada, Sport, and Corsa—gave a progressively more track-focused feel to the power curve, shift speed, stability control settings, damper response, and even the tiller if the optional Lamborghini Dynamic Steering was present.

The latter technology, a carryover from Audi, would prove to be a controversial addition. Dynamic Steering uses aerospace-derived technology to vary the steering ratio and powered assistance according to speed. Rather than a conventional rack, the steering column feeds in to a "harmonic drive" in which an electrically driven elliptical inner rotor alters the shape of a sunwheel attached to the input shaft. This acts on another ring gear fixed to the output shaft, with the relative movement altering the effective steering ratio.

This system gives light steering with fewer turns from lock to lock at parking speeds, while adding more weight and becoming less direct on the open road, thereby reducing the tendency to fidget that a linear-rack car might display. It's light and

Each Huracán is suspended from a cradle as it passes along the assembly line and approaches completion; this helps to shield it from damage.

compact and requires little power, and promises a subtle level of "intervention" when the stability control systems detect a slide. But in practice Dynamic steering is not to all tastes, and many drivers—this author included—dislike the strangely elastic feel it transmits as you turn the wheel, even though the actions of the system are claimed to be "virtually imperceptible."

To give customers a choice, adaptive magnetorheological damping would be offered as an option, as on the forthcoming Audi R8 with which the Huracán would share platform and drivetrain. As the final phases of development got underway, one of the priorities for Lamborghini's engineers was to ensure that the two cars were noticeably different—and hopefully, with the pride of Sant'Agata at stake, the Huracán being the better of the two. One benchmark laid down from Ingolstadt was for it to hit 200 miles per hour at Nardo without becoming unstable. Early prototypes added to chief test driver Giorgio Sanna's sum of gray hairs but, as Reggiani would later attest proudly, when the Audi bigwigs arrived for the final sign-off, the final prototype Huracán hit all its high-speed marks—and did so without requiring a pop-up rear spoiler such as those seen on McLaren's 12C and (perhaps more significantly) the Audi R8 and TT. The final shape also produced 3 percent less drag than the already clean Gallardo.

Getting to that point required substantial wind tunnel work, smoothing out some of the more outré details of the original proposals. Still, Perini pronounced himself happy: "We have a solid body with really strong elements, clean surfaces, and precise lines. The design proposal was tested from the beginning to have the perfect performance in driving and downforce. It's very interesting how the design of this car can be extreme and usable.

"We have tried to hide all the openings that are necessary for the cooling system, and for aerodynamic performance, in a carefully shaped and clean volume. There are hexagonal designs around the side opening; it's a feature that we like, a DNA that is arriving from the Aventador. We love to work with this kind of geometrical line."

Hexagonal shapes predominated on the finished Huracán, starting with the front air intakes. Here Perini left the shapes open, with the lower inner legs halting before they met the nose. A pair of creases on the hood, starting at the bottom corners of the windscreen and tracking inwards, also flattened out before they met the tip of the nose. Taken as a whole with the angular headlamps that enclose Y-shaped white LEDs, the effect was like the toothy maw of the titular creature in the movie Predator. The hexagonal theme continued in the graphic of the side windows, with the angles reflected in the two air intakes on each flank, rounded off with a honeycomb-style panel between the Aventador-style rear lights. Twenty-inch wheels properly filled the arches and gave an aggressive, ready-to-pounce stance.

The Huracán's launch process began with a teaser website called the Hexagon Project, which went live in November 2013. Tellingly, this offered no images of the forthcoming car, nor did it suggest what it would be called. Visitors could listen to a recording of the new V-10 and log their email address for more updates, and that was it. As a data-capture exercise and anticipation builder, it could not have been more effective; pity the poor marketing executives who had to trawl through the many thousands of contact details to sort the bona fide sales leads from the excitable teenagers.

Studio photographs of the finished car were released to selected media the following month, along with confirmation of the car's name, previously rumored to be Cabrera. The big moment would be the unveiling at the Geneva show, superintended by company president Stephan Winkelmann. "This," he told attendees, "is a new chapter."

Lamborghini had taken more than 1,000 orders for the car ahead of its launch, but the reaction to the new shape was not uniformly positive. McLaren F1 designer—and sometime Lamborghini engineering consultant—Peter Stevens declaimed it as "a chaotic mess of lines."

Since most car nuts, including those opening their wallets for a new Huracán, begged to differ, Lamborghini could afford to let this kind of criticism pass. Its executives were probably more concerned about activities within the Volkswagen Group tent: Dr. Hackenberg manifested himself frequently during the press launch activities like

(Continued on page 206)

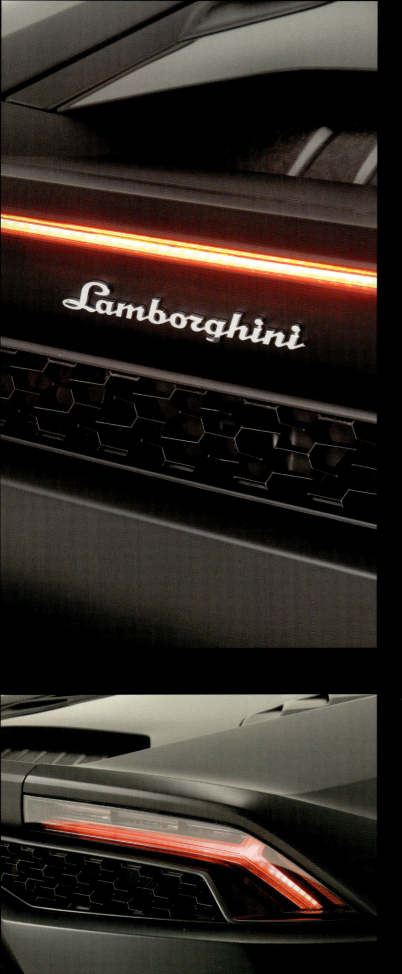

Huracán LP610-4

Chassis	Aluminum/carbon fiber spaceframe
Suspension	Independent double wishbones front/rear, coaxial coil springs, telescopic self-adjusting shock absorbers, anti-roll bars, and anti-squat bars
Brakes	Ventilated Brembo discs with ABS, ASR, and ABD
Wheelbase	2620 mm
Front/rear track	1668 mm/1620 mm
Wheels/Tires	20 in × 8.5 in, Pirelli PZero 245/30 (front); 20 in × 11 in, Pirelli PZero 305/30 (rear)
Engine	Rear longitudinal-mounted 90-degree V-10
Bore/Stroke	84.5 mm/92.8 mm
Cubic capacity	5204 cc
Compression ratio	12.7:1
Maximum power	602 bhp at 8250 rpm
Valve gear	Dual overhead camshafts, chain drive, 4 valves per cylinder, continuously variable timing
Fuel/ignition system	Bosch MED engine management with direct and indirect injection systems
Lubrication	Dry sump
Gearbox	7-speed LDF dual-clutch
Transmission	Four-wheel drive with electrohydraulic multi-plate clutch
Dry weight	1422 kg
Top speed	202 mph

Based on the LP610-4, the Huracán Performante introduced active aerodynamics – including a forged-composite rear wing – and a new version of the V-10 engine, offering 29 bhp more.

(Continued from page 201)

a Dickensian specter, availing himself of every opportunity to remind the audience of how much Audi DNA lay under the skin—not, one presumes, the body, detail, or tenor of the message Lamborghini wanted to transmit.

At such events there is only so much jaw-jaw the average motoring writer can take before they want to grab the keys and run, and the Huracán launch was no exception. For all the talk of DNA, Audi or otherwise, the key questions had to be laid down on the road: what was the Huracán experience like?

Sampling a Huracán for the first time at Portugal's Ascari circuit, experienced hand Georg Kacher wrote in *Car* magazine:

> Although this Lamborghini can bark louder than most of the rivalling big dogs, its personality is much more mature and less aggressive than the Gallardo. One case in point concerns the new Lamborghini Doppia Frizione dual-clutch gearbox which bites faster and harder than the rather rough automated manual fitted to the Gallardo, yet at the same time can be totally fluent, seamless and relaxed. But dictating the pace with your fingertips is still the most rewarding modus operandi. Revs permitting, the transmission will change down several gears at a time while you keep the paddle pulled.

In Corsa mode, the steering action speeds up dramatically, tip-in is an object lesson in preemptive obedience, upshifts are accompanied by a whiplash domino effect, torque vectoring clearly favors the rear wheels, and the shock absorbers keep the body almost level even under hard braking and through maximum-g corners. Initially, stability control provides exactly that and a bit too much of it, but after about 20 laps when the tires start to melt and the car fishtails out of second- and third-gear bends, the calibration feels suddenly spot-on. By that point, the carbon-ceramic brakes are hot enough to decelerate our gleaming citrus fruit on wheels with such time warp efficiency that it seemed perfectly okay to hit the pedal eerily late, even though extreme deceleration would occasionally trigger an initial wobble or two.

Not only a sharper and faster driving machine, but also a more compliant and accessible sports car. Even more so than the Aventador, it is two cars in one.

As befits the most accomplished supercar Lamborghini has made, the Huracán wildly exceeded sales expectations, taking just five years to reach the number of units the Gallardo sold in ten. The 14,022nd car off the line, an Evo coupe finished in matte grey (Grigio Titans in the catalog) went to a buyer in Korea in 2019. Lamborghini cleverly fleshed out the range, offering not only a Spyder version of the original LP 610-4, but also a more affordable two-wheel-drive version, the LP 580-2, in both open-top and coupe versions. It also followed the fashion for track-oriented specials, launching the LP 640-4 Performante at Geneva in 2017 and following it with a Spyder variant a year later. The Super Trofeo race series, in which professionals are paired up with amateur racers, transitioned seamlessly from the Gallardo to the Huracán in 2015 with the release of the LP 620-2 Super Trofeo, a properly stripped-out race car in which the V-10 was tuned up to 612 brake horsepower.

Mitja Borkert gently waved his pencil over the exterior design for a mid-cycle refresh, but it was the work underneath that properly merited the revised model's official Evo nomenclature. Let us begin with the engine—the uprated 631-brake-horsepower version of the V-10 introduced in the Performante model, featuring titanium inlet valves and a lightweight exhaust system. As a signal of intent, this was unequivocal. The Evo also introduced a four-wheel steering system similar to that which proved so transformative in the Aventador, along with the new multiplex, unified electronic vehicle and engine control system, Lamborghini Dinamica Veicolo Integrata. Under this new regime, the traction control, magnetic suspension, and even the much-maligned Direct Steering were greatly improved.

Huracán Evo

Chassis	Aluminum/carbon fiber spaceframe
Suspension	Independent double wishbones front/rear, coaxial coil springs, telescopic self-adjusting shock absorbers, anti-roll bars, anti-squat bars
Brakes	Carbon-ceramic with 6-piston calipers front, 4-piston calipers rear
Wheelbase	2620 mm
Front/rear track	1668 mm/1620 mm
Wheels/Tires	20 in × 8.5J, Pirelli PZero 245/30 ZR20 (front); 20 in × 11J, Pirelli PZero 305/30 ZR20 (rear)
Engine	Rear longitudinally mounted 90-degree V-10
Bore/Stroke	84.5 mm/92.8 mm
Cubic capacity	5204 cc
Compression ratio	12.7:1
Maximum power	640 bhp at 8000 rpm
Valve gear	Dual overhead camshafts, chain drive, 4 valves per cylinder, continuously variable timing
Fuel/ignition system	Bosch MED engine management with direct and indirect injection systems
Lubrication	Dry sump
Gearbox	7-speed LDF dual-clutch
Transmission	Haldex IV four-wheel drive
Dry weight	1422 kg
Top speed	202 mph

While comparing the Evo slightly unfavorably with McLaren's class-leading 720S in terms of steering and brake feel, refinement, and everyday useability, *Autocar* magazine's Simon Davis homed in on the Evo's unique appeal: "But the McLaren lacks the character of the Lamborghini, the Huracán Evo is a proper supercar, with a properly endearing feral streak and an engine to die for. The 720S might be the one you'd want to live with, and it might even be the more capable of the two on the track, but we reckon it's the Lamborghini you'd go to bed and dream about."

Naturally a Spyder variant followed, as did a two-wheel-drive version 73 pounds lighter than the standard model, but with the engine detuned to 602 brake horsepower. While there are those who feel that less cannot be more, and that a modern supercar is incomplete without all-wheel drive and a supercomputer superintending the traction and suspension, the Huracán Evo RWD is a remarkably compelling package. "With little lost in terms of performance or driver appeal, the RWD seems like a no-brainer," wrote Antony Ingram in *Evo* magazine, "even if the list price is less of a deciding factor in this segment of the market than it might be further down."

At the other end of the range, and perhaps with a view to the coming necessity of hybridization, in 2021 Lamborghini introduced the Super Trofeo Omologato, the most flamboyant iteration of the Huracán yet. Pitched as a (barely) road-legal version of the Super Trofeo race car, its exterior is a riot of racing cues—from the periscope engine air intake to the Le Mans prototype-style shark fin and dramatic rear diffuser. The fin is reckoned to improve yaw stability during high-speed cornering and improve the conditioning of the airflow to the rear wing, but on a car such as this, where it appears nobody in Centro Stile was prepared to say "no," it could simply be there just for the sake of it. Seventy-five percent of the body panels are carbon fiber. "The STO is to track days what musical theater is to acting," wrote Tom Ford in *Top Gear* magazine. "A bit OTT, but joyous, raucous and fun."

If this is the end of the line for the naturally aspirated V-10, it is undoubtedly exiting with a flourish and leaving the audience craving more.

Mitja Borkert refreshed the Huracán's styling for the Evo model, but the majority of the changes were under the skin: the updated 631bhp V10 introduced in the Performante was mated to a new, integrated electronic control system, four-wheel steering joined the package, and there was an even a rear-wheel-drive-only version for purists.

HURACÁN STERRATO

When the Huracán Sterrato was unveiled as a concept in 2019, it was widely regarded as the answer to a question nobody had asked: "What would an off-road version of the Huracán look like?" With a wider track, higher profile tires, 43 millimeters more ground clearance, and a more rear-biased all-wheel-drive system, the Sterrato (which translates as "dirt road") is best imagined as a modern take on the rallying Porsche 911 rather than a rival to the Land Rover genre.

While the concept car was originally believed to be a guerilla project cooked up by Mitja Borkert and engineer Rouven Mohr, evading the scrutiny of the VW board, it was uncannily convincing when tested in real life. "They had to remove me from the hot seat with a blow torch," wrote the usually reserved Georg Kacher.

At the time of publication, prototype models have been photographed undergoing cold-weather testing in northern Europe, suggesting a production run may happen before the Huracán reaches the end of its model cycle.

Automobili Lamborghini

THE LEVIATHANS

INTRODUCING

RISING TENSIONS IN THE MIDDLE EAST AND ELSEWHERE during the 1970s created a potential demand for a new generation of fast-attack military vehicles to replace the venerable Jeep and its ilk: something faster, more agile, more capable of evading or resisting the latest ordnance. Surely Lamborghini, the supercar maker with roots in agricultural machinery, possessed the skill set to develop such an offering, right?

THE "RAMBO LAMBO"

Lamborghini demonstrated the Cheetah prototype (above, left) in 1977 but it was nearly a decade before the definitive LM002 (above, right) was ready for sale. Military customers remained cool on the idea but celebrities and rogues loved it.

A decade, two sets of owners, and a bankruptcy separated the company's first dabbling in this sector and the finished item. Yet, the product never gained great traction in its intended market, but it did appeal to a very different constituency.

Lamborghini unveiled the Cheetah, a co-production with the US military contractor Mobility Technology International, at the Geneva motor show in 1977. Powered by a rear-mounted waterproofed 5.9-liter Chrysler V-8, the project was a nonstarter. Doubts abounded over whether the rear-biased weight distribution made it fit for purpose, the partners were threatened with legal action for IP infringement by the maker of a rival design, and Lamborghini was sliding toward insolvency.

Under the Mimran administration, the company returned to the idea with a revised version of the design, the LM001, shown at Geneva in 1981. Still rear-engined, it failed to enthuse potential clients. A third pass at the concept would right many of the wrongs.

Unveiled in 1982, the LMA002 ("A" for *anteriore* since the engine was now at the front, "LM" possibly for Lamborghini Militaria or Lamborghini Mimran, though no documentation exists to support either claim fully) definitively prefigured the production model. The new 4.8-liter version of Lamborghini's V-12, as used in the Countach LP500S, replaced the US-sourced V-8, and its new location naturally required an all-new spaceframe chassis design, enabling Lamborghini to accommodate ten people rather than the original four. The bodywork remained angular, enabling the option of armor plating. Still, military customers decided to pass, perhaps wary of the maintenance demands of an engine sourced from an exotic Italian sports car.

As the booming global economy fed an era of irrational exuberance, the LM concept would finally have its day. In 1986, Lamborghini took the covers off a substantially revised prototype, now badged the LM002, at the Brussels motor show. Under restyled but still angular bodywork, the car now boasted the latest 5.2-liter V-12 from the Countach Quattrovalvole; as a concession to possible uses in far-flung places, the compression ratio was reduced to enable it to run on lower-octane fuel. While still rugged, the interior offered far more concessions to comfort and featured more luxurious trim.

The LM002, quickly nicknamed "the Rambo Lambo" after the movie character played by Sylvester Stallone, provided a perfect statement vehicle for those who wished to announce their arrival in a certain manner. The first production vehicle was sold to the king of Morocco. Stallone himself acquired one, as did a gallery of royalty, rocks stars, and rogues, including Pablo Escobar, who used his to patrol his infamous Hacienda Nápoles estate, which included a private zoo.

More than 300 LM002s are believed to have been built, making it one of Lamborghini's most successful models of the era—as well as a precursor to the modern trend for sport-utility vehicles. Its spiritual successor would prove transformative for the company.

LM002

Chassis	Steel spaceframe
Suspension	Independent double wishbones front/rear, coil springs, telescopic shock absorbers
Brakes	Ventilated discs (front), drums (rear)
Wheelbase	3000 mm
Front/rear track	1615 mm/1615 mm
Wheels/Tires	17 in × 11 in, Pirelli Scorpion 325/17
Engine	Front-mounted 60-degree V-12
Bore/Stroke	85.5 mm/75 mm
Cubic capacity	5167 cc
Compression ratio	9.5:1
Maximum power	450 bhp at 6800 rpm
Valve gear	Dual overhead camshafts, chain drive, 4 valves per cylinder
Fuel/ignition system	6 Weber carburetors, twin pump, electronic ignition
Lubrication	Wet sump
Gearbox	ZF 5-speed
Transmission	4-wheel drive with limited-slip differential
Clutch	Dry single-plate, hydraulically assisted
Dry weight	2700 kg
Top speed	130 mph

Just as many Porsche devotees are conflicted over the existence of the Cayenne and Macan SUVs, which they feel have diluted the brand's cachet, long-standing Lamborghini aficionados have a complex relationship with the Urus. Under the Volkswagen Group's custodianship, the marque's finances have stabilized, its model line has been bolstered, and the quality of its engineering and manufacture has consistently improved. And yet sales volumes remained modest even into the early part of the past decade, hovering around the 2,000-units-per-year mark. The Urus, introduced as a concept car at the 2012 Beijing Auto Show—a significant choice of location given the promise of the Chinese market—intended to double that figure. Thus far, it has overachieved. Having launched the car in December 2017, Lamborghini built its 15,000th example in July 2021.

At launch, Lamborghini described the Urus as the world's first super SUV. Pragmatism has been the key to the car's runaway success, at a cost of the brawny eccentricity that characterized the LM002. In styling the 2012 concept, Filippo Perini riffed off the dramatically folded edges and brooding presence of his Aventador design; the production car signed off by Perini's successor, Mitja Borkert, differed only in details so far as the exterior was concerned. Judiciously using proven items from the VW parts bin enabled Lamborghini to develop the Urus cost-effectively and bring it to market with nothing that might scare off potential buyers. The MLB-Evo platform also provides the basis for the Cayenne, Audi Q8, and Bentley Bentayga SUVs. While rumors abounded that the concept featured the Gallardo's V-10,

Lamborghini remained tight-lipped—and the final car was powered by a 640-brake-horsepower version of Audi's 4-liter twin-turbo V-8, driving through an eight-speed automatic gearbox.

The result was a car that carried less Sant'Agata DNA than some might prefer, but that nevertheless delivered on the majority of the touchpoints one would expect of a 21st-century Lamborghini. Its brash styling made its stablemates seem jejune by comparison, and the V-8's state of tune (thanks to reprofiled cylinder heads and cams, along with new turbos) enabled it to comfortably see off Audi's sportiest G8 in most performance benchmarks, though both are electronically limited to a top speed of 155 miles per hour.

To keep the show on the road, Lamborghini head of R&D Maurizio Reggiani raided the full arsenal of the VW Group's inventory. Active anti-roll bars, rear-wheel steering, a Torsen center differential, and torque vectoring on the rear diff enable the Urus to lay down that 640 brake horsepower in a manner that defies its height and weight. The air suspension offers a choice of three ride heights in combination with different settings for the damping, plus variable response from the powertrain and the steering. There's a variety of separate modes for riding on asphalt and various other surfaces, including snow, gravel, and sand, all controlled from the center console.

Whether Urus owners use the full gamut of these functions is open to question, but the positive for Lamborghini is that there is a huge and growing number of Urus owners to which you could direct such an enquiry.

Urus

Chassis	Unitary steel/aluminum based on VW MLB Evo platform
Suspension	Independent adaptive air suspension with electromechanical active roll stabilization
Brakes	Ventilated carbon-ceramic discs
Wheelbase	3003 mm
Front/rear track	1695 mm/1710 mm
Wheels/Tires	21 in × 9.5 in Pirelli P Zero 285/21 (front); 21 in × 10.5 in Pirelli P Zero 315/21 (rear)
Engine	Front longitudinally mounted twin-turbo V-8
Bore/Stroke	86 mm/86 mm
Cubic capacity	3996 cc
Compression ratio	9.7:1
Maximum power	650 bhp at 6000 rpm
Valve gear	Dual overhead camshafts, belt drive, 4 valves per cylinder
Fuel/ignition system	Direct fuel injection, electronic ignition
Lubrication	Wet sump
Gearbox	ZF 8-speed automatic
Transmission	4-wheel drive with limited-slip differential and dynamic torque distribution
Clutch	Dry single-plate, hydraulically assisted
Dry weight	2200 kg
Top speed	177 mph

TO THE FUTURE PAST

REMAKE,

more costly to obtain and less socially acceptable to burn in profligate quantities? There is a finite quantity of efficiency gains a performance car manufacturer can find through lightweighting.

RE-IMAGINE, REBOOT

At the 2014 Paris Motor Show, the world got its first glimpse of what a hybrid-powered Lamborghini might look like. Company President Stephan Winkelmann described the Asterion as a "technology demonstrator." More significant, perhaps, were the lengths Winkelmann went to manage expectations and establish distance from the newly released McLaren P1 and Porsche 919 hybrid supercars, saying the Asterion was "conceived more for comfortable luxury daily cruising than for ultimate track performance."

Based on the Aventador's monocoque, the Asterion's composite two-door coupé bodyshell certainly had more in common with the Urraco and its descendants than the Huracán from which it took its V-10 engine, supplemented by three brushless electric motors that brought the car's theoretical peak power to 898 brake horsepower. Feather-footed drivers could accomplish in the region of 67 miles per gallon given the right circumstances, and the Asterion's CO_2 emissions were rated at 98 grams/kilometer, which compared favorably with the Aventador's 370 grams/kilometer.

A year later, Lamborghini admitted it had canned plans to develop the car into a production model and would be ploughing resources into the Urus instead. Winkelmann cited lukewarm customer reaction.

Based on Aventador underpinnings, the Asterion could have been a modern take on the Urraco—but Lamborghini shelved the idea after showing the concept in 2014, deciding to retain focus on ultra-high-performance cars.

"They told us that they were open to innovation, including hybrid technology, but only if it came with the benefit of added performance," he said. "A Lamborghini super-sports car is driven maybe 3,000 miles (4,828 kilometers) a year, not every day, so the electrification has to offer an added intensity to justify its inclusion."

Packaging certain elements of the hybrid powertrain had been a problem—the lithium-ion battery pack was shoehorned into the tunnel that would normally house the forward-driving propshaft in the Aventador. Lamborghini never confirmed the Asterion's weight but did say the hybrid system added 551 pounds to the overall package. Winkelmann's comments seemed to indicate a vision for the company in which Lamborghini's brand proposition rested entirely on high performance; there would be no descent from this high altitude, no return to the mid-market epitomized by the Urraco, or to the world of the elegant and understated grand tourer. Given the disappointing sales of those models, it's hardly surprising the current custodians of the Lamborghini brand don't see the point in going there. Neither will there be a new Espada. At the 2008 Paris Motor Show, Lamborghini unveiled the Estoque (named after the short sword used by matadors to deliver the killing blow), a four-door sedan with a front-mounted Gallardo V-10. However, plans for production never passed the feasibility study stage.

A four-door Lamborghini sedan? Demonstrated at the 2008 Paris Motor Show, the Estoque had a front-mounted V-10 sourced from the Gallardo.

And yet the issue of electrification remains live, as it were, even when servicing an ultra-wealthy demographic for whom Lamborghinis are low-mileage toys. During the decade just past, jitters set in at board level within several high-performance car manufacturers as the upstart electric-vehicle company Tesla began to cannibalize their sales, offering buyers the key differentiator of being able to signal virtue alongside advanced technology. The response was a series of high-profile EV hypercar concepts, mostly just a set of arbitrary performance benchmarks wrapped in eye candy.

Lamborghini's pitch in this arena was suitably dramatic, but it elevated itself above its peers because it genuinely hinted at workable electrified Lambos to come. The Terzo Millennio—"third millennium"—was developed in conjunction with the prestigious Massachusetts Institute of Technology and unveiled there in 2017. Mitja Borkert's first clean-sheet Lamborghini design was an appropriately startling announcement, improbably low and wide, blending race-style aerodynamic concepts with modern hypercar tropes such as the tapered keel and flying buttresses.

"The car must have a wow factor," Borkert said. "Otherwise we have failed."

Much of the car's spec remains highly theoretical. Its intended performance benchmark was to hit a maximum speed of 186 miles per hour and be capable of doing at least three hot laps of the Nürburgring Nordschleife. Rather more interesting was Lamborghini's proposed route toward achieving this target: rather than the chassis in effect placing the occupants on top of a large and heavy lithium-ion battery cell, it would power its four electric motors via superconductors. While costly and difficult

to engineer, superconductors are capable of higher energy density than traditional batteries, are lighter, and can charge and discharge faster. The ongoing partnership with MIT was aimed at developing technologies through which copper anodes and cathodes could be woven into the carbon-fiber structure, in effect making the bodywork and chassis part of the battery system. There was talk, too, of developing aerospace-style polymers to give the bodywork a self-healing capacity.

While much of the technology espoused by the Terzo Millennio concept remains over the immediate horizon, it was clear supercapacitors offered a solution to the packaging, weight, and power-discharge limitations imposed by standard batteries. At the Frankfurt motor show in 2019, Lamborghini revealed the Sián FKP 37, its most powerful road car ever, capable of accelerating from rest to the benchmark 62

The Terzo Millennio concept car introduced Lamborghini's collaboration with MIT on high-tech materials, along with an electric drivetrain powered by high-discharge supercapacitors rather than conventional batteries.

miles per hour in 2.8 seconds and topping out at 220 miles per hour, propelled by an Aventador SVJ powertrain augmented by a supecapacitor-fed electric motor within the transmission.

While the Sián's name refers to Bolognese argot for a bolt of lightning, its furniture nods to the company's history—FKP being the initials of the late Ferdinand Karl Piéch (the visionary engineer who was at the head of the Volkswagen Group when it acquired Lamborghini), born in 1937. The production run of 63 examples refers to the Lamborghini car company's own birth date and, in common with late-period Lambos of this rarefied ilk, every one was sold to collectors and regular customers before it was even unveiled—despite costing in the region of $3.3 million once local taxes were applied and individual tailoring by Lamborghini's Ad Personam program factored in. Should you wish to construct your own mechanized effigy, even the Lego Technic model is eye-wateringly expensive.

Somewhat disappointingly, beneath the Terzo Millennio–inspired carbon-fiber skin, the Sián is identical to the Aventador SVJ, with the exception of the hybrid system. Even the interior is similar. Since the electric power is fed to all four wheels, and partially directed toward smoothing the gaps between upshifts, it's only when the driver selects the track-oriented "Corsa" driving mode and requests manual gearchanges that the Sián becomes a proper monster.

"Then, and only then mind, does the Sián begin to feel like it might just be worth the outrageous amount it costs," wrote former TVR racer Steve Sutcliffe in *Auto Express*. "The Sián is a slightly cynical car in that it has made Lamborghini a small fortune in the process, despite not costing that much more than an Aventador to make, but in reality, it's far from just a marketing exercise. It's actually a sensational car to drive, one that contains tech that will help keep the big, characterful and unhinged V12 Lamborghinis going for a good few years to come. As enthusiasts, we can't help but love it for that."

Lamborghini subsequently revealed an open-top version of the Sián—permanently open at that, for it doesn't even have a targa lid—featuring an identical powertrain and, remarkably for such a vehicle, no loss of aerodynamic performance compared with the roofed model. The rear deck features individual roll hoops for each occupant and, cleverly, active cooling vanes that ameliorate the drag caused by the roof aperture, only opening when the engine and exhaust temperatures reach a certain level. Only 19 were built and, naturally, sold before the car was unveiled.

This wasn't the first time Lamborghini had leveraged the Aventador to create a super-profitable limited-run model, nor would it be the last before the Aventador is replaced. At the 2016 Geneva show, the company marked the 100th anniversary of Ferruccio Lamborghini's birth with the Centenario, a carbon-fiber special edition limited

Lamborghini's Sián, named after the Bolognese dialect term for a bolt of lightning, is the company's most powerful road car ever. An Aventador SVJ-based powertrain combined with a supercapacitor-fed electric motor within the transmission delivers a claimed top speed of 220 mph.

FOLLOWING PAGES: The open-top Sián has no roof at all and features active cooling vanes which mitigate the drag induced by the open cockpit. It's claimed to offer identical aerodynamic performance to the closed-roof model.

Limited to 20 Coupés and 20 Roadsters, the 2016 Centenario marked the 100th anniversary of Ferruccio Lamborghini's birth. Underneath the dramatic composite skin, it was based on the Aventador SV.

to 20 coupés and 20 roadsters. Both the monocoque and the aggressively sharp bodywork were formed in the lightweight composite material, enabling Lamborghini to offset the weight gain from the addition of a rear-wheel steering system that would later be deployed in the Aventador SVJ. The four-wheel-drive powertrain was donated by the Aventador SV, but with extra tuning to yield 759 brake horsepower.

Mining the company history with a view to turning it into a profit center has required what specialists in managementese might euphemistically describe as "a pivot." Back in 2006, the company displayed the Miura Concept, Walter de Silva's first work as head of design. Based around Murciélago underpinnings, the car was ostensibly intended to celebrate the 40th anniversary of the Miura's unveiling and was a passion project for the design chief, who claimed to have dreamed of reinterpreting the original's design cues through a modern prism.

Stephan Winkelmann was unequivocal that Lamborghini remained a future-focused company and that neither this nor any other rose-tinted nostalgia product would enter production. "The Miura was a celebration of our history," he said. "Retro design is not what we are here for. So we won't do the Miura, even as a limited edition."

Come 2021 and the 50th anniversary of the Countach, that undertaking had been quietly consigned to the memory hole. Lamborghini's Polo Storico historic division briefly delighted enthusiasts with a loving recreation of the original LP 500 prototype,

an undertaking that required 25,000 hours of labor. Mitja Borkert's design team used photographs of the original and 3D scans of chassis 001 (in Lamborghini's museum) to create an accurate envelope in which the mechanicals were handcrafted from original blueprints. The attention to detail extended to engaging Pirelli to reproduce period-spec Cinturato CN12 tires.

The sticking point? The car was destined for the private collection of an unnamed high-net-worth individual who had approached Lamborghini in 2017 to suggest (and underwrite) the project.

Lamborghini had already confirmed it was disinterring the Countach name for a new limited-edition model, based on the Aventador chassis but with an 800-brake-horsepower hybrid four-wheel-drive powertrain derived from the Sián. It was revealed during Monterey Car Week in August 2021, by which time the entire 112-car run had sold out, because Lamborghini had been phoning its best customers beforehand (as per established tradition with these limited-edition bulls when the quantity built is a cherry-picked figure from history, in this case the Countach's original project designation of LP112). At $2.5 million for the base model, $3 million if you ticked all the options, the Countach LPI 800-4 is nothing if not rarefied . . . and divisive. *Road & Track* magazine summed up the industry's thoughts pithily, describing it as a "cynical cash grab aimed at ultra-wealthy collectors."

Although the Countach LPI 800-4 (above and opposite) scandalized original Countach designer Marcello Gandini, the entire production run sold out immediately.

OPPOSITE: Lamborghini's racing division, Squadra Corse, now offers bespoke cars to high-net-worth individuals and the SC20 (opposite, top) is its second such example. Based on the Aventador SVJ chassis and drivetrain, it was designed by Mitja Borkert to the customer's brief: "Just make it look cool."

Among those infuriated was Marcello Gandini, who had participated in an interview with Borkert in June, believing the purpose was to discuss the creation of the original car as part of the 50th anniversary celebrations. When the video of the interview was bundled into the LPI 800-4 announcement, Gandini, believing himself to have been ambushed, took the extraordinary step of issuing a statement to disassociate himself from the scheme.

"I have built my identity as a designer, especially when working on supercars for Lamborghini, on a unique concept: each new model I would work on would be an innovation, a breaker, something completely different from the previous one. Courage, the ability to create a break without sticking to the success of the previous car, the confidence in not wanting to give in to habit were the very essence of my work. It is clear that markets and marketing itself has changed a lot since then, but as far as I am concerned, to repeat a model of the past, represents in my opinion the negation of the founding principles of my DNA."

The imminent replacements for the Huracán and Aventador will give Lamborghini's Centro Stile a platform to establish the brand's forward-looking credentials again, visually at least. From an engineering perspective, they will be more conservative. Downsizing, turbocharging, and full electrification are rubicons Lamborghini feels unable to cross without alienating its customer base. Tightening emissions legislation worldwide will make this a challenging path to navigate. By 2024, the entire model lineup will be hybridized, most likely with conventional batteries rather than supercapacitors, which do not provide the requisite reduction in CO_2. There may yet be a full EV, but not until the end of the decade.

Can you imagine a Lamborghini without a mighty V-12? Nor can the people who make them.

INDEX

Advanced Composite Structures Laboratory, 183
Alboreto, Michele, 109
Alfieri, Giulio, 68, 69, 72, 75, 78, 84, 86
Alliot, Philippe, 109
Amelia Island Concours d'Elegance, 28
American Motors Corporation, 101
Anderson, Gregory, 126
Artese, Alexandro, 68
ATS 2500GT, 22
ATS racing, 16, 32
Audetto, Daniele, 109
Audi, 105–106, 114, 115, 116, 117, 121, 122, 132–133, 134, 144, 183, 197, 198, 199, 206
Austin 1100, 28
Autódromo Internacional Nelson Piquet, 109
Automobili Ferruccio Lamborghini SpA, 10, 18. See also Automobili Lamborghini SpA; Nuova Automobili Ferruccio Lamborghini SpA
Automobili Lamborghini Advanced Composite Structures Laboratory, 183
Automobili Lamborghini SpA, 13, 32, 61, 62, 67, 68–69, 92. See also Automobili Ferruccio Lamborghini SpA; Nuova Automobili Ferruccio Lamborghini SpA
Aventador. See also Lamborghini models
 Aventador J, 174, *174*
 Aventador LP700-4 Roadster, 166, *166–167, 168–171*
 Aventador LP720-4 50th Anniversario, 173
 Aventador LP720-4 50th Anniversario Roadster, 173
 Aventador LP750-4 Superveloce, 173, 175
 Aventador LP770-40 SVJ, 175
 Aventador SC18 Alston, 177
 Aventador SC20, 177, *237*
 Aventador S Coupé, *172*
 Aventador S LP740-4, *173*, 174, 175, 176
 Aventador S Roadster, *173*
 Aventador SV, *170*
 Aventador SVJ Roadster, *164–165*, 169
 Aventador SVJ SC18 Alston, 177
 design of, 160, 161
 pictured, *160, 163, 164–165, 166–167, 168, 169, 170, 171, 172, 173, 174, 177*
 pricing of, 168, 171, 174
 reception of, 162, 168
 specifications, 166, 172

Bailoni, Louis, 102–103
Balboni, Valentino, 7, 32, 96, 100, 120, 124, 141
Baraldini, Franco, 82, 83
Barker, John, 124, 144
Barlow, Jason, 168
Barry, Ben, 176
Bernard, Eric, 109
Bertone, Nuccio, 19, 23, 26, 36, 57
Bertone of Turin, 23, 24, 25, 28, 36, 45, 52, 59, 60, 82, 86, 115, 121, 132
Bizzarrini, Giotto, 11, 12, 16, 24, 32, 36, 120, 175
Bizzarrini 5300 Strada, 16
BMW
 5-Series, 19
 M1, 68, 83
Boeing, 183
Bologna Motor Show, 103
Bolster, John, 44
Bonnet Djet, 22
Borkert, Mitja, 175, 176, 177, 207, 212, 228
Brabham, Jack, 32
Brussels motor show, 27, 217

Cage, Nicolas, 37
Camoradi racing team, 32
Capellini, Luigi, 82
Carrozzeria Marazzi, 48, 52, 58
Carrozzeria Touring, 11, 13, 23, 48, 61, 136
Casner, Lloyd "Lucky," 32
Ceccarani, Massimo, 104, 120, 133
Centro Stile design department, 121, 132, 150, 161, 210, 236
Chilton, Chris, 124, 173
Chiti, Carlo, 32, 36
Chrysler, 75, 78, 92, 96, 97, 100, 101, 102, 104, 108, 109, 115, 132, 216
Citroen BX, 19, 96
Citroen SM, 75
Cizeta Moroder V-16, 96
Coltrin, Peter, 25, 59
Cosworth Technology, 36, 144
Countach. See also Lamborghini models
 Countach 25th Anniversary, *70–71*, 72–73, 76, 78
 Countach 5000 Quattrovalvole, 72–73, *76–77*, 78
 Countach Evoluzione, 78
 Countach LP400, 62, *64–65*, 66, 68
 Countach LP400S, 79
 Countach LP500, 58, 59, 60, *60, 61, 234–235*
 Countach LP500S, 72, 79, 216
 Countach LPI 800-4, 235–236, *236, 237*
 Countach prototype, 58, 60, 61, 62, 63
 design of, 18, 19, 32, 36, 53
 pictured, *58, 60, 61, 63, 64–65, 66, 67, 69, 70–71, 72, 73, 74–75, 76–77, 78*
 pricing of, 66–67
 prototype, 58, 60, 61, 62, 63
 reception of, 66
 specifications, 65, 76
 200 mph mark, 72–73
Courage, Piers, 36

Dallara Automobili, 36
Dallara, Gian Paolo, 11, 12, 13, 18, 21, 22, 23, 24, 26, 27, 28, 29, 32, 36, 45, 59, 68, 82
Dalmas, Yannick, 109
Davis, Miles, 31
Davis, Simon, 210
Dennis, Ron, 109
Deschamps, Marc, 86
De Tomaso, Alejandro, 75
De Tomaso company, 28, 36, 82
De Tomaso models
 Mangusta, 27, 58
 Vallelunga, 22
Detroit Auto Show, 122
Diablo. See also Lamborghini models
 Diablo 6.0, 107
 Diablo GT, 106
 Diablo GTR, 106
 Diablo SE, 99
 Diablo SE30, 103
 Diablo SV, 103, 106
 Diablo VT, 102, *104–105*, 106–107, *110–111*
 Diablo VT Roadster, 93, *94–95*, 106
 pictured, *93, 94–95, 96, 98, 100, 101, 102, 104–105*
 reception of, 98, 106–107
 specifications, 95, 99, 111
Di Capua, Vittorio, 104, 105
Djody, Setiawan, 102, 103
Donkerwolke, Luc, 115–116, 132
Dron, Peter, 73
Dutch Grand Prix, 36

engines
 Bizzarrini V-12, 11–12, 22, 27, 97, 160, 175
 F1 V-12, 108–109
 Gallardo V-10, 123, 124, 134, 140, 144, 197, 227
 L539 V-12, 175
 Murciélago LP640, 125
 Murciélago Roadster and, 120
 Reventón Roadster SV, 155

Ferrari, 16, 32, 123, 135, 144, 175, 190, 191
 246 Dino, 52
 308 Dino, 55
 308GTB, 86
 360 Modena, 132, 133
 365 GTB/4 "Daytona," 58
 458 Italia, 168, 196
 599: 126
 F40, 91, 98
 F430, 136
Ferrari, Enzo, 8, 9, 10, 22, 36, 146
FIA GT Championship, 106, 124, 146
Fiat X19, 19
Fitzgerald, Manfred, 155
Ford, Henry, II, 22
Ford, Tom, 141, 210
Ford GT40, 24
Ford Motor Company, 68, 144
Forghieri, Mauro, 108, 109
Formenti, Federico, 48
Formula 1 racing, 12, 16, 32, 36, 37, 48, 68, 73, 75, 101, 108–109, 159, 174
Frankel, Andrew, 162
Frankfurt Motor Show, 106, 109, 154, 229

Gale, Tom, 97
Gallardo. See also Lamborghini models
 Corsa mode, 141
 design of, 121, 132
 Gallardo Balboni special edition, 141
 Gallardo LP550-2, 141, 145, 147, *147*
 Gallardo LP560-4, 140–141, *142–143*, 143
 Gallardo LP570-4, 141
 Gallardo SE, 136
 Gallardo Spyder, 136, *137*, 141,
 Gallardo Spyder Performante, 141
 Gallardo Superleggera, 136–137, 140, 141
 pictured, *130–131, 133, 134, 137, 138–139, 142–143, 145, 146, 147*
 racing, 146
 reception of, 135, 136, 137, 140
 specifications, 138, 143, 147
Gandini, Marcello, 18, 19, 23, 24, 27, 28, 44, 45, 48, 53, 57, 58, 60, 62, 91, 96, 97, 102, 103, 115, 236
Geneva motor show, 13, 23, 24, 25, 26, 27, 29, 43, 45, 48, 52, 60, 62, 66, 69, 86, 102, 103, 115, 122, 132, 134, 136, 140, 144, 174, 190, 201, 207, 216, 231
George, Simon, 120
Giugiaro, Fabrizio, 132
Giugiaro, Giorgetto, 19, 23–24. See also Italdesign
GLAS (Gonzalez Luna Associates) consortium, 109

Hahne, Hubert, 37
Hakkinen, Mika, 109
Hoberg, Dominik, 150
Hughes, Mark, 30
Huracán. See also Lamborghini models
 Huracán Evo, 207, 210, *211*
 Huracán LP 580-2, 207
 Huracán LP 610-4, 205, *205*, 206, 207
 Huracán LP 620-2 Super Trofeo, 207
 Huracán LP 640-4 Performante, 206, 207, *207, 208–209*
 Huracán LP 640-4 Spyder, 207
 Huracán Sterrato, 212, *212, 213*
 Huracán Super Trofeo Omologato, 210
 pictured, *194–195, 200, 201, 202–203, 204, 205, 208–209, 211*
 reception of, 201, 206–207
 specifications, 205, 210

Iacocca, Lee, 92, 102
IDEA, 121, 132
Ingram, Antony, 210
International Lead Zinc Research Organization, 28
Iso, 16
Italdesign, 103, 115, 121, 132. See also Giugiaro, Giorgetto

Japanese Lamborghini Owners Club, 146
Japanese SuperGT series, 146
J.P. Morgan bank, 101

Kacher, Georg, 206–207, 212
Kimberley, Mike, 103, 104
Kott, Douglas, 123
Krupp-Drauz, 134

Lamborghini, Ferruccio, 8, 9–10, 11, 12, 13, 16, 18, 22–23, 24, 26, 28–29, 36, 37, 43, 44, 45, 48, 52, 53, 57, 58, 59, 60, 62, 67, 82, 146, 231
Lamborghini, Tonino, 62
Lamborghini Blancpain Super Trofeo, 146, 153
Lamborghini Bruciatori SpA, 10
Lamborghini Engineering, 108, 109
Lamborghini models. See also Aventador; Countach; Diablo; Gallardo; Huracán; Miura; Murciélago
  250GT, 9, 11, 16
  250GTO, 16
  350GT, 11, 12, 13, *13*, 14, 15, 16, *19*, 21, 26, 32, 36, 127
  350GTV, 12
  400GT, *14*, 15, 16, 25, 43, 58
  400GT 2+2, 16, 18, 45
  Asterion, 226–227, *226, 227*
  Canto, 115, 116, *117*
  Centenario, 231, 234, *234*
  Cheetah prototype, 216, *216*
  Egoista, 182, *182*
  Espada, 19, 27, 44, 45–46, *45, 46, 47,* 47, 48, 52, 58, 60, *227*
  Estoque, *228*
  Islero, 44, 48, *49, 50–51,* 51, 52, 58
  Jalpa, 69, 75, 86, *86, 88–89,* 89, 96, 115
  Jarama, 29, 52, *52,* 54, 58, 60
  LM002, 216–217, *216, 217, 218,* 219, *219*
  Marzal, 27, 43, 44, *44,* 45, 46
  P140, 96, 101, 105
  Reventón, 140, 150, 152–154, *156–157,* 157
  Reventón Roadster, 150, *150,* 151, *151,* 154–155
  Sesto Elemento, 152, 179–180, *178–179, 180, 181,* 183–185, *183, 184, 185, 186–187, 188, 189, 192–193* 193
  Sián FKP 37, 229–231, *231, 232–233*
  Silhouette, 82–84, *82, 83, 84,* 85
  Terzo Millennio, *228,* 229, *230*
  Urraco, 18, 19, 29, 52–53, *54,* 55, *55,* 58, 60, 61, 62, 66, 67, 69, 81, 82, 83, 226, 227
  Urus, 220–221, *220, 221, 222,* 223
  Veneno, 177, 182, *190*
Lamborghini Oleodynamica SpA, 10
Lamborghini Tractori SpA,
Lancia Stratos, 19
Lancia Stratos Zero, 60
Larini, Nicola, 109
Larrousse, Gerard, 108, 109
Leimer, Rene, 62, 67, 68, 83
Luna, Fernando Gonzalez, 109
Lutz, Bob, 109

Mackenzie, Angus, 114
Marchesi of Modena, 45, 67
Marmiroli, Luigi, 72, 96, 97, 104
Martini, Pierluigi, 73

Maserati, 32, 36, 68, 75, 135
  250F, 75
  Bora, 58, 75
  Khamsin, 75
  Merak, 75
  Tipo 61 "Birdcage," 32
McLaren, 32, 108, 109, 159, 184, 191
  12C, 168, 196, 199
  720S, 210
  P1, 226
McNally, Patrick, 48
Mille Miglia road race, 10
Mimran brothers, 68, 69, 75, 78, 86, 91, 92, 216
Miura, Eduardo, 24
Miura. See also Lamborghini models
  design of, 18, 19, 23, 24
  Miura Concept, 234
  Miura P400, 22, 33, *33*
  Miura P400S, 27–28, *34–35,* 35
  Miura P400SV, 29, *38–39,* 40, 41, *41*
  Miura Roadster, 26, 28, *28*
  Miura S Jota, 37, *37*
  Miura SVJ, 37
  pictured, *20–21, 22, 23, 26, 28, 30, 31, 33, 34–35, 38–39, 40, 41*
  roofless, 27–28, *28*
Modena Team, 109
Mohr, Rouven, 212
Moroder, Giorgio, 96
Munoz, Emilio, 160
Murciélago. See also Lamborghini models
  design of, 115–116
  Murciélago 40th anniversary model, 123
  Murciélago LP640, 124, *125,* 125, *126*
  Murciélago LP650–4 Roadster, 127
  Murciélago LP 670–4 SuperVeloce China Limited Edition, 127
  Murciélago LP670–4 SV, 126–127, 129
  Murciélago R-GT, 124
  Murciélago Roadster, 121, 122–123
  Murciélago Versace edition, 126
  pictured, *112–113, 114, 115, 116, 117, 118–119, 121, 122, 125, 126, 128*
  specifications, 119, 125, 129

Neckarsulm (Audi) facility, 134
Nichols, Mel, 83
Novaro, Emile, 96
Nuova Automobili Ferruccio Lamborghini SpA, 69, 92. See also Automobili Ferruccio Lamborghini SpA; Automobili Lamborghini SpA

Ohlson, John, 32
Oliver, Ben, 136
Orsi, Adolfo, 75

Paris Motor Show, 179, 226, 227
Perini, Filippo, 161, 168, 174, 196, 200, 220
Petrucco, Carlo, 109
Phillips, John, 116, 122
Phillips, Roger, 83
Piëch, Ferdinand, 105, 115, 116, 230
van de Poele, Eric, 109
Porsche
  911: 52, 107, 132, 212
  917: 105
  919: 226
  959: 91
  Targa-top, 82
Putra, Hutomo "Tommy" Mandala, 102

Reggiani, Maurizio, 144, 175, 184, 197, 199, 221
Reiter Engineering, 124, 146
Renault Supercinq, 19
Reti, Zoltan, 68
Robinson, Aaron, 135

Robinson, Peter, 98, 100, 101, 133
Rossetti, Georges-Henri, 62, 67, 68

S.A.M.E group, 62
Sackey, Joe, 27, 31
Sant'Agata Bolognese facility, 11, 25–26, 29, 45, 61, 67, 68, 75, 83, 92, 96, 101, 103, 107, 108, 113, 115, 120, 133, 134, 144, 150, 152, 183, 199
Sargiotto, 11, 13
Scaglione, Franco, 11
Scuderia Serenissima, 32
Senna, Ayrton, 108, 109
Setright, L. J. K., 12, 24, 27
Sgarzi, Ubaldo, 25, 26
Shah Pahlavi (Shah of Iran), 37
Sielaff, Stefan, 182
de Silva, Walter, 182, 234
Società Autostar, 16
Squadra Corsa, 146
Stanzani, Paolo, 11, 18, 22, 24, 28–29, 36, 48, 52, 53, 59, 61, 62, 67–68
Stevens, Peter, 103–104, 115, 201
Stroppa, Piero, 24
Suárez, Hugo Banzer, 60
Sutcliffe, Steve, 137, 231
Suzuki, Aguri, 109

Targa Florio road race, 62
Taylor, Michael, 153
Torres, Juan José, 61
Trintignant, Maurice, 32
Trott, Nick, 168
Turin motor show, 12, 21, 22, 23, 24, 53, 55, 58, 60, 82

Vivian, David, 126–127
Volkswagen Group, 105, 121, 197, 201, 220, 230
Volpi di Misurata, Count, 16, 32

Wallace, Bob, 12, 13, 22, 27, 32, 36, 37, 53, 61, 62, 67–68
Webster, Larry, 106
Williams, Frank, 36
Winkelmann, Stephan, 32, 150, 168, 174, 182, 183, 196–197, 201, 226, 227, 234
Wolf, Walter, 68
World War II, 9

Zagato, 16, 103, 115